Moonlit Beginnings: Spell craft and Rituals for Lunar Novices

A Practical Handbook for Moon Magic

Daniel Reynolds

© Copyright 2024 - All rights reserved.

The content contained within this book may not be reproduced, duplicated or transmitted without direct written permission from the author or the **publisher.**

Under no circumstances will any blame or legal responsibility be held against the publisher, or author, for any damages, reparation, or monetary loss due to the information contained within this book, either directly or indirectly.

Legal Notice:

This book is copyright protected. It is only for personal use. You cannot amend, distribute, sell, use, quote or paraphrase any part, or the content within this book, without the consent of the author or publisher.

Disclaimer Notice:

Please note the information contained within this document is for educational and entertainment purposes only. All effort has been executed to present accurate, up to date, reliable, complete information. No warranties of any kind are declared or implied. Readers acknowledge that the author is not engaging in the rendering of legal, financial, medical or professional advice. The content within this book has been derived from various sources. Please consult a licensed professional before attempting any techniques outlined in this book.

By reading this document, the reader agrees that under no circumstances is the author responsible for any losses, direct or indirect, that are incurred as a result of the use of information contained within this document, including, but not limited to, errors, omissions, or inaccuracies.

Table of Contents

INTRODUCTION 5
CHAPTER I. Understanding Lunar Energy 7
The Significance of the Moon in Various Cultures 7
The Moon's Influence on Earth 10
Harnessing Lunar Energy for Magic 14
CHAPTER II. Moon Phases and Their Meanings 19
New Moon: Beginnings and Intentions 19
Waxing Crescent to Full Moon: Manifestation and Growth..... 23
Waning Gibbous to New Moon: Release and Renewal 29
CHAPTER III. Moonlit Tools and Altar Setup 33
Essential Tools for Moon Magic 33
Creating a Sacred Space 37
Altar Decor and Symbolism 42
CHAPTER IV. Lunar Correspondences 47
Moon in Zodiac Signs 47
Moon in Astrological Houses 53
Aligning Spells with Lunar Phases 58
CHAPTER V. Moonlit Spells for Everyday Magic 64
Love and Relationships 64
Prosperity and Abundance 69
Protection and Cleansing 74
CHAPTER VI. Rituals for Each Moon Phase 79

New Moon Ritual for Setting Intentions 79

Full Moon Esbat Rritual for Manifestation 83

Waning Moon Ritual for Letting Go 87

CHAPTER VII. Moonlit Divination 92

Lunar Tarot Spreads 92

Scrying by Moonlight... 95

Dream Interpretation and Moon Magic 99

CHAPTER VIII Crafting Moon Elixirs and Potions 103

Infusing Water with Lunar Energy 103

Moon-Enhanced Herbal Brews 106

Creating Moonlit Oils and Salves 110

CHAPTER IX. Moonlit Celebrations and Festivals 115

Honoring Lunar Deities 115

Seasonal Moon Festivals 119

Hosting Your Own Moonlit Gatherings 123

CONCLUSION 127

INTRODUCTION

"Moonlit Beginnings: Spellcraft and Rituals for Lunar Novices" is an enchanting and practical handbook designed to illuminate the mystical realm of moon magic for those venturing into the captivating world of spellcraft. Authored with a seamless blend of wisdom and accessibility, this e-book serves as an indispensable guide for novices, offering a gateway to harnessing the potent energies of the moon.

As the moon has long been revered across diverse cultures as a symbol of magic, intuition, and cyclical transformation, "Moonlit Beginnings" unveils the secrets of lunar influence and empowers readers to embark on their spiritual journey. The e-book begins by laying a foundation of understanding, demystifying the phases of the moon and its unique energies. Through insightful explanations, readers profoundly comprehend how lunar cycles intersect with various aspects of life.

The heart of the handbook lies in its hands-on approach to moon magic. Through meticulously crafted spells and rituals, even those new to the art can embark on a transformative odyssey. From simple yet potent rituals to more intricate spellcraft, each chapter is a stepping stone, guiding novices toward a deeper connection with the moon's energies.

Moreover, "Moonlit Beginnings" goes beyond mere instruction, encouraging readers to personalize their practice. The e-book provides a canvas for individual exploration, inviting novices to infuse their unique essence into each ritual. Aspiring practitioners will find a wealth of knowledge, from creating sacred spaces to selecting appropriate crystals and herbs to enhance the efficacy of their moon-centric endeavors.

In essence, "Moonlit Beginnings" is a guide and a companion for those seeking to awaken the magic within themselves. With its empowering insights and practical tools, this e-book opens the door to a world where the moon becomes a luminary guide on the transformative path of spellcraft and ritualistic exploration.

CHAPTER I

Understanding Lunar Energy

The Significance of the Moon in Various Cultures

The moon's silvery glow and ever-changing phases have captivated human imagination across diverse cultures throughout history. Its significance transcends geographical boundaries, weaving through the tapestry of myth, religion, and folklore. In countless civilizations, the moon has been revered as a celestial deity, a cosmic guide, and a symbol of cyclical renewal. This section explores the multifaceted significance of the moon in various cultures, unraveling the threads that connect humanity's collective fascination with this celestial luminary.

The moon was pivotal in the religious and cultural landscape in ancient Mesopotamia. The Sumerians, among the earliest civilizations, worshipped the moon god Nanna. Revered as the son of the sky god An and the earth goddess Ki, Nanna was believed to govern the cycles of time and the tides. The lunar calendar, devised by the Sumerians, not only marked the passage of months but also influenced the development of later lunar calendars in other cultures.

Moving eastward to ancient China, the moon became integral to Taoist philosophy and Chinese folklore. Chang'e, a lunar goddess, is a central figure in Chinese mythology. She is said to have flown to the moon after ingesting the Elixir of Immortality. The Mid-Autumn Festival celebrates this tale, sometimes called the Moon Festival, where families gather to view the full moon, eat mooncakes, and recognize the symbolic togetherness symbolized by the lunar deity.

The ten white horses in Chandra's chariot represent the moon's phases. The ebb and flow of life's fortunes is symbolically associated with the waxing and waning of the moon. Hindu women celebrate Karva Chauth by fasting and praying for their husbands' health and longevity. Traditionally, they break their fast when they see the moon.

Lunar symbolism associated the moon with Thoth, the god of writing and wisdom, was also prevalent in ancient Egypt. Because the lunar calendar fell on the same day the Nile flooded every year, it was crucial to agriculture. Moreover, Egyptian cosmology associated the waxing and waning of the moon with the life cycle, signifying the cyclical nature of birth, death, and rebirth.

Across the ancient Americas, the moon held profound significance for indigenous cultures. In the traditions of the Lakota Sioux, the moon is revered as Grandmother Moon, a wise and nurturing presence. Native American tribes often structured their calendars based on lunar cycles, with ceremonies and rituals aligned to the moon's phases. The Cherokee, for example, marked the new moon with ceremonies for healing and renewal.

In classical mythology, the Roman goddess Luna, equivalent to the Greek Selene, embodied the moon's ethereal radiance. Luna's chariot, drawn by two horses, traversed the night sky, illuminating the world below. The Romans celebrated the festival of Lunalia in her honor, a time for feasting and acknowledging the moon's benevolent influence.

Turning to the Abrahamic religions, the moon carries symbolic weight in Judaism, Christianity, and Islam. In Judaism, the lunar calendar regulates the observance of festivals, with the new moon, or Rosh Chodesh, marking the beginning of each month. The lunar cycle determines the Sabbath and other celebrations, reinforcing the sacred connection between the Hebrew calendar and the moon.

In Christianity, the moon is indirectly linked to the determination of Easter, based on the ecclesiastical approximation of the spring equinox. Biblical verses often use lunar imagery to convey spiritual meanings, such as Psalm 104:19, which poetically describes the moon as a marker of the seasons.

Within Islam, the lunar calendar plays a central role in determining the Islamic months, with Ramadan, the month of fasting, commencing with the sighting of the new moon. The crescent moon, known as the "hilal," holds particular importance, marking the beginning of Islamic months and serving as a visual symbol of the Islamic calendar.

The moon's influence extends to folklore and superstitions, shaping cultural practices and beliefs. The full moon is often associated with werewolves and other supernatural phenomena in European traditions. The term "lunatic" itself, derived from the Latin word "lunaticus," meaning "moonstruck," reflects historical associations between the moon and madness. Despite these superstitions, the moon has also inspired poets, artists, and dreamers, with its radiant glow evoking a sense of mystery and wonder.

In Japanese culture, the moon takes on a poetic and contemplative role. The tradition of "Tsukimi" or moon-viewing involves gatherings to appreciate the full moon, particularly during the autumn harvest season. This cultural practice reflects a deep connection to nature and the changing seasons, as well as an acknowledgment of the transient beauty of life.

Scientific exploration has demystified many aspects of the moon in modern times, yet its cultural significance endures. In the 20th century, we witnessed a giant leap for humanity with the Apollo moon landings, further fueling fascination and admiration for Earth's celestial companion. The iconic image of the Earthrise, as seen from the moon and captured during the Apollo 8 mission, became a symbol of interconnectedness and environmental awareness.

In conclusion, the significance of the moon in various cultures is a testament to the universal human experience of gazing at the night sky and finding meaning in celestial rhythms. From ancient mythologies to contemporary scientific endeavors, the moon continues to be a source of inspiration, reflection, and cultural richness. Its influence transcends time and borders, reminding us of the shared human fascination with the luminous orb that graces our night sky.

The Moon's Influence on Earth

The Moon, Earth's only natural satellite, profoundly influences our planet across various dimensions, ranging from gravitational interactions to cultural symbolism. This section delves into how the Moon shapes and influences Earth, exploring scientific phenomena, cultural significance, and the historical context that binds these celestial bodies in a cosmic dance.

Scientifically, the most apparent impact of the Moon on Earth is gravitational. The oceans bulge under the Moon's gravitational pull during its cycle around the Earth, producing high tides that face the Moon and an opposite set that meets the other way. Tidal motion, the regular rise and fall of sea levels, is a crucial natural phenomenon affecting marine life, coastal ecosystems, and even human activities like fishing.

The Moon's gravitational pull affects Earth's oceans and induces a slight deformation of the Earth's shape. This phenomenon, known as Earth's axial precession, causes a gradual wobble in the planet's rotation axis over time. The Moon's gravitational influence and the Sun's contribute to this precession, impacting the orientation of Earth's poles and the timing of equinoxes and solstices. While these changes occur over vast time scales, they underscore the intricate celestial mechanics that govern Earth's motions and seasons.

Beyond gravitational forces, the Moon's influence extends to Earth's atmosphere. Although the Moon has no atmosphere of its own, its gravitational pull affects the Earth's atmosphere, particularly at the edges of the atmosphere where it meets space. This gravitational interaction results in a phenomenon known as atmospheric tides. While these tides are much weaker than oceanic tides, they contribute to the complex dynamics of Earth's atmospheric circulation.

The Moon's impact is not limited to the physical realm; it extends into human societies' cultural and symbolic dimensions. Throughout history, the Moon has held profound significance in mythology, folklore, and religious beliefs. In various cultures, the Moon is personified as a deity, representing life cycles, death, and rebirth. The waxing and waning of the Moon have been metaphorically linked to the ebb and flow of human experiences, influencing rituals, celebrations, and spiritual practices. In ancient Mesopotamia, the Sumerians worshipped the moon god Nanna, who governed time and tides. The lunar calendar devised by the Sumerians guided agricultural activities and became a cultural touchstone, influencing subsequent civilizations. Similarly, in Hindu mythology, the Moon is personified as Chandra, a god associated with beauty and enlightenment. The lunar phases symbolize the cosmic dance of creation and destruction, reflecting Hindu cosmology's cyclical nature of existence.

Chinese folklore, rich with lunar symbolism, venerates the goddess Chang'e, who resides on the Moon. The Mid-Autumn Festival celebrated across East Asia, revolves around the full moon and honors familial unity, with families gathering to appreciate the moon's radiance. In Islamic traditions, the lunar calendar dictates the timing of religious observances, with the crescent moon marking the beginning of each month. Ramadan, the month of fasting, commences with the sighting of the new moon, exemplifying the intersection of lunar cycles with religious practices.

In Western cultures, the Moon has been a muse for poets, artists, and philosophers. Its silvery glow and mysterious allure have inspired countless works of literature and art. The concept of a "man on the moon" and various lunar deities permeate Western mythology, contributing to a cultural fascination that persists today. Furthermore, the association of the full moon with mystical phenomena, such as werewolves and witches, has left an indelible mark on Western folklore and popular culture.

Scientific exploration in the modern era has deepened our understanding of the Moon's influence on Earth. The Apollo missions, initiated by NASA in the 1960s and 1970s, marked a historic milestone in human space exploration. These missions produced the first human footprints on the lunar surface and yielded crucial scientific information. Astronauts' return-transported moon rocks provided information on the Moon's composition, geological past, and place in the more extensive solar system.

The Moon's influence on Earth extends to the field of astrobiology. Scientists consider the Moon a natural celestial body that has witnessed Earth's biological evolution. Lunar rocks, devoid of an atmosphere, provide a unique record of solar wind and cosmic rays, offering a glimpse into the conditions that prevailed in the early solar system. Studying the Moon's history allows scientists to infer the environmental changes on Earth and understand the factors that facilitated the emergence and sustenance of life.

In addition, the Moon is used as a celestial laboratory to test fundamental physics theories. Scientists could determine the exact distance between Earth and the Moon thanks to experiments carried out during the Apollo missions, such as installing retroreflectors. These experiments yield essential information that helps us better comprehend spacetime and gravitational dynamics.

In the 21st century, renewed interest in lunar exploration has emerged, with government space agencies and private companies planning missions to establish a sustained human presence on the Moon. These endeavors aim to expand our scientific knowledge and explore the Moon's potential resources, such as water ice, which could support future space exploration and serve as a stepping stone for missions to Mars and beyond.

In conclusion, the Moon's influence on Earth is a rich tapestry woven from scientific phenomena, cultural symbolism, and human exploration. From shaping the tides that sculpt our coastlines to inspiring artistic and spiritual expressions, the Moon occupies a central role in the human experience. As we continue to unravel the mysteries of our celestial companion through scientific exploration and cultural appreciation, the Moon remains a luminous testament to the interconnectedness of Earth and the cosmos.

Harnessing Lunar Energy for Magic

The concept of harnessing lunar energy for magical practices is deeply rooted in ancient traditions and mystical beliefs, transcending cultural boundaries to weave a tapestry of lunar magic that spans centuries. Across diverse civilizations, the moon has been revered as a celestial force with transformative powers, influencing everything from tides and agricultural cycles to human emotions and spirituality. This section explores the mystical realm of harnessing lunar energy for magic, delving into moon magic's historical, cultural, and contemporary aspects as a potent and revered form of metaphysical practice.

The moon was often revered and incorporated into religious practices in ancient civilizations. The moon's waxing and waning cycles were seen as symbolic representations of birth, death, and rebirth. In Mesopotamia, the Sumerians worshiped the moon god Nanna, attributing governance over time and tides to him. The lunar calendar, devised by these ancient astronomers, became crucial for agricultural planning and ceremonial observances. Similarly, in ancient Egypt, the moon held significance in religious rites, where lunar cycles were integrated into the farm calendar to align with the annual flooding of the Nile.

The link between lunar phases and magical practices persisted through various cultures. Selene personified the moon in ancient Greece, representing its ethereal beauty and influence. The Greeks believed in the magical properties of moonlight, associating it with inspiration, dreams, and night's enchantment. This connection between the moon and the mystical realm is further reflected in the Greek goddess Hecate, often depicted as a triple deity associated with the new moon, full moon, and dark moon phases, symbolizing the stages of life, death, and rebirth.

The Roman tradition also embraced lunar deities, with Luna holding a prominent place in their pantheon. Luna, the goddess of the moon, was revered for her role in illuminating the night sky. The Romans celebrated Lunalia, a festival dedicated to Luna, with rituals and ceremonies conducted to invoke her benevolent energy. The lunar influence extended into Roman folklore, where the moon was believed to govern women's fertility and menstruation cycles.

Moving eastward, ancient China embedded lunar magic into its cultural and spiritual practices. The Chinese believed in the yin and yang energies, with the moon representing the yin, which is associated with receptivity, intuition, and femininity. Taoist traditions embraced moon gazing to connect with celestial energies and harness the moon's transformative powers. The ancient Chinese also observed the lunar calendar, utilizing it for agricultural activities and traditional festivals, such as the Mid-Autumn Festival, a celebration of the full moon's beauty and symbolic reunion of families.

In Hinduism, the moon is significant in mythology and ceremonial practices. The lunar god Chandra is considered the embodiment of beauty, grace, and creativity. The waxing and waning of the moon are metaphors for the cyclical nature of life and the pursuit of spiritual enlightenment. Hindu festivals, like Karva Chauth, involve rituals that harness lunar energy, with fasting and prayers conducted by women to seek the well-being and longevity of their spouses, often concluding with the sighting of the moon.

Lunar magic found its way into diverse indigenous cultures as well. Native American tribes structured their ceremonies and rituals around lunar cycles, recognizing the moon as a guiding force in their spiritual practices. The Lakota Sioux, for example, hold sacred ceremonies during the full moon, acknowledging Grandmother Moon as a source of wisdom and guidance. Similarly, the Cherokee people attribute healing properties to the moon, conducting ceremonies during specific lunar phases to harness its mystical energies.

The medieval European tradition was deeply influenced by blending pagan practices with emerging Christian beliefs—the medieval grimoires, books containing instructions for rituals and spells, often incorporated lunar correspondences and timings. The idea of moon phases influencing magical workings became entrenched in Western occultism, with the full moon considered a time of heightened magical energy and manifestation.

During the Renaissance, the revival of interest in ancient wisdom and esoteric traditions further fueled the exploration of lunar magic. Alchemists and mystics sought to harness the transformative energies of the moon to unlock the secrets of the universe. The concept of sympathetic magic, where like attracts like, was applied to lunar magic, with practitioners aligning their intentions with the corresponding lunar phases for optimal results. In folk magic and witchcraft, lunar energy played a pivotal role. Witches and cunning folk believed that the moon's phases influenced the potency of their spells and rituals. The waxing moon was associated with growth and manifestation, making it an ideal time for spells to attract love, wealth, or success. Conversely, the waning moon was suitable for banishing rituals, removing obstacles, or releasing negative energies. The full moon, with its peak energy, was viewed as a powerful time for divination, charging magical tools, and performing rituals of heightened intensity.

The modern revival of interest in witchcraft and contemporary pagan practices has seen a resurgence of lunar magic. Wicca, a modern pagan religious movement, strongly emphasizes the cycles of the moon. Many Wiccans celebrate Esbats, monthly rituals conducted during the full moon, where they commune with lunar energies, cast spells, and perform divination. The Wiccan Wheel of the Year, a cycle of eight seasonal festivals, incorporates lunar phases as practitioners attune their magical workings with the ever-changing face of the moon.

Modern witchcraft practitioners often create lunar altars adorned with symbols, crystals, and representations corresponding to the moon's phases. The distinct magical aims of each lunar phase can frame spellwork and ritual planning. For instance, the full moon is best for empowerment and manifestation, and the new moon is thought to be a time for making intentions and fresh starts.

Crystals and gemstones are integral to lunar magic and are believed to amplify and channel lunar energies. Moonstone, associated with the lunar goddesses, is revered for its reflective qualities and connection to intuition. Named for the moon goddess Selene, selenite is thought to improve psychic and spiritual perceptions. Practitioners frequently charge their crystals in the full moon's light to give them additional magical properties. Herbs and plants also play a crucial role in lunar magic.

Different lunar phases are believed to influence the potency of herbs, with practitioners harvesting or utilizing specific plants based on the moon's cycle. Sp cultivated with plants corresponding to the moon's energy, Lunar gardens become sacred spaces for magical workings. Herbs like mugwort, associated with lunar energy and dreams, are often used in rituals to enhance psychic abilities and visionary experiences.

Moonwater, water charged under the moon's light, is a lunar magic staple. Practitioners collect water during specific lunar phases, imbuing it with the moon's energy. Moonwater is then used for ritual purification, consecration of magical tools, and anointing during spells.

The idea is to capture the essence of the moon's energy in the water, creating a potent and versatile magical tool.

The lunar calendar guides lunar magic practitioners by showing when specific magical operations are most effective. Each of the eight phases of the moon cycle—new moon, waxing crescent, first quarter, waxing gibbous, full moon, waning gibbous, last quarter, and declining crescent—has corresponding energies and magical meanings. Understanding these stages allows practitioners to align their intentions with the natural cycles of lunar energy.

While the mystical allure of lunar magic is steeped in tradition, contemporary practitioners continue to innovate and adapt these ancient practices. The rise of online communities, books, and workshops has facilitated sharing knowledge and experiences among those exploring lunar magic. Social media platforms serve as virtual covens where practitioners connect, share rituals, and collectively celebrate the moon's magic.

In conclusion, harnessing lunar energy for magic is a rich and enduring tradition transcending time and cultural boundaries. The moon's effect on magical practices has always been a source of power and inspiration for people involved in magic, from ancient civilizations to contemporary witchcraft and pagan communities. Through customary practices, current modifications, or the investigation of particular associations with the moon, people persistently discover meaning in the ethereal domain of lunar sorcery, integrating their goals into the cosmic trance of the lunar orb.

CHAPTER II

Moon Phases and Their Meanings

New Moon: Beginnings and Intentions

The new moon, a celestial phenomenon marking the beginning of a lunar cycle, has been revered across cultures as a potent and auspicious time for new beginnings and setting intentions. This section delves into the significance of the new moon, exploring its spiritual, cultural, and metaphysical dimensions as a symbol of renewal and manifestation. The new moon has traditionally been connected to renewal, introspection, and the beginning of life-changing activities.

In various mythologies and spiritual traditions, the new moon represents a cosmic reset or the moment when the moon starts its journey afresh and gradually waxes to brighten the night sky. People can create personal transformations during the new moon since this cyclical pattern reflects the ups and downs of life. The moon was adored as a heavenly body connected to life and death cycles by ancient cultures like the Greeks and Romans. Greek mythology held that the energy of the new moon, which embodies the possibility of fresh stars, was represented by the lunar goddess Selene. Similarly, the Romans commemorated the new moon as a representation of Luna's restorative power over the night sky.

The connection between the new moon and renewal is further exemplified in Hindu mythology, where the lunar god Chandra is associated with regeneration cycles. The waxing and waning of the moon in Hindu cosmology symbolize the eternal dance of creation and dissolution, reinforcing the new moon's significance as a catalyst for fresh starts. In Chinese folklore, the new moon is linked to the rejuvenation of energies, aligning with the yin aspect of the yin-yang philosophy. The yin, representing receptivity and the feminine, is mirrored in the new moon's symbolic blank canvas—a time when intentions can be sown and nurtured.

Cultures across the globe have incorporated the new moon into their calendars and rituals. The Jewish tradition, for instance, marks the beginning of each month with the appearance of the new moon. Rosh Chodesh, celebrating the new moon, is a time for reflection, prayer, and setting intentions for the month ahead. In Islam, the lunar calendar governs religious observances, and the sighting of the new moon marks the beginning of each Islamic month. This moment is particularly significant during the holy month of Ramadan, emphasizing the spiritual importance of the new moon in initiating sacred practices.

In magic and metaphysics, the new moon is a fertile period for setting intentions and planting seeds for future manifestations. Many practitioners of magic and witchcraft align their workings with the lunar cycles, recognizing the unique energies associated with each phase. With its symbolic blank slate, the new moon is an ideal time for individuals to focus on their desires, goals, and aspirations. This period is often associated with introspection, allowing individuals to identify what they wish to manifest.

New moon rituals vary across magical traditions, but common themes include intention-setting meditation and symbolic acts of creation. Practitioners may engage in rituals such as candle magic, where the flame represents the spark of intention, or crystal charging, harnessing the energy of selected stones to amplify intentions. Writing down intentions on paper, often as a new moon manifestation list, is a prevalent practice, grounding one's desires in tangible form. As the moon begins its waxing phase, these intentions are believed to gain momentum and energy, aligning with the natural forces of the universe.

Crystals associated with new moon energy, such as clear quartz and moonstone, are often used in rituals during this phase. Clear quartz, known as a versatile amplifier, is thought to enhance the potency of intentions, while moonstone, connected to lunar energies, is believed to promote intuition and receptivity. These crystals are cleansed and charged under the new moon's influence, imbuing them with the energy of fresh beginnings.

Herbs and plants also play a role in new moon rituals, with practitioners selecting botanical allies associated with intention-setting and initiation. Herbs like sage, Lavender, and frankincense may be used for smudging or as ingredients in rituals, enhancing the energetic atmosphere and providing a sensory backdrop for manifestation practices. Aromatherapy, often incorporated into new moon rituals, utilizes the power of scents to evoke specific energies conducive to intention-setting and reflection.

In astrology, the new moon represents a conjunction of the sun and moon, aligning their energies in a particular zodiac sign. This astrological placement adds a layer of nuance to the new moon's influence, as each zodiac sign is associated with distinct qualities and themes. Individuals often consult astrological charts to gain insight into the specific energies of a new moon, tailoring their intentions to align with the astrological sign in which the new moon occurs. For example, a new moon in Aries might inspire intentions related to assertiveness, courage, and new ventures. In contrast, a new moon in Pisces may encourage intentions focused on intuition, creativity, and spiritual pursuits.

The "dark moon" concept is sometimes used interchangeably with the new moon, although some traditions distinguish between the two. The dark moon is considered the period immediately preceding the new moon when the moon is completely invisible in the night sky. Some practitioners view the dark moon as a time for deep introspection, shadow work, and releasing old patterns before the new moon heralds the beginning of fresh intentions. This nuanced approach recognizes the subtle shifts in energy during the transition from the dark moon to the new moon.

In the contemporary spiritual and self-help landscape, the new moon has become a focal point for intention-setting practices. The accessibility of information and the rise of social media platforms have facilitated sharing new moon rituals and manifestation techniques. Online communities, workshops, and guided meditations centered around the new moon have created a virtual space for individuals to come together, collectively harnessing the power of intention during this lunar phase.

Integrating technology and spirituality has led to the development of new moon apps, providing users with information on lunar phases, astrological alignments, and guided rituals tailored to each new moon. These digital tools offer a modern twist to age-old practices, making lunar magic more accessible globally. Individuals can receive notifications, join virtual gatherings, and participate in guided ceremonies from the comfort of their homes, fostering a sense of community and shared intention.

Critics argue that the commercialization and popularization of new moon rituals risk diluting the depth and authenticity of these practices. While social media platforms showcase visually appealing rituals and aesthetically pleasing altars, the essence of personal connection and intention-setting can be overshadowed.

Striking a balance between the modern convenience of digital platforms and the nature of genuine, heartfelt intention is a challenge for those navigating the contemporary landscape of lunar magic face.

In conclusion, the new moon's symbolism of renewal and fresh beginnings holds a timeless and universal appeal. Whether viewed through mythology, spirituality, or contemporary metaphysics, the new moon is a cosmic canvas upon which individuals can inscribe their aspirations and intentions. As cultures and spiritual practices evolve, the essence of the new moon remains a source of inspiration, inviting individuals to participate in the eternal dance of creation and manifestation under the celestial glow of the lunar cycle.

Waxing Crescent to Full Moon: Manifestation and Growth

The journey from the waxing crescent to the full moon in the lunar cycle is a time of profound energetic transformation, symbolizing the stages of manifestation, growth, and fruition. This period, marked by the moon's increasing illumination, holds significance in various spiritual, magical, and cultural traditions. As the moon progresses through its phases, from the slender crescent to the radiant full orb, it reflects the cyclical nature of life, offering a symbolic structure for individual and group development. This section explores the waxing crescent to complete the moon phase, unraveling its symbolic richness and delving into how it has been interpreted and harnessed across different cultures and mystical practices.

The waxing crescent, the initial phase after the new moon, marks the commencement of the moon's journey toward full illumination. Scientifically, this phase unfolds as the sun's rays progressively illuminate a more significant portion of the moon's surface visible from Earth. Metaphorically, the waxing crescent is often associated with the germination of intentions set during the new moon. It is a time when the seeds of desire begin to sprout, and individuals may feel a subtle but palpable surge of energy propelling them forward. In various mythologies, the waxing crescent is akin to the first stirrings of life—a moment pregnant with potential.

In magical and metaphysical traditions, the waxing crescent phase is an opportune time for amplifying intentions, casting spells for growth, and setting the stage for manifestation. Practitioners align their magical workings with the increasing energy of the waxing moon, utilizing this period to infuse their desires with the momentum needed for realization. Rituals during this phase often involve activities like candle magic, where each day sees the lighting of a candle symbolizing the gradual growth of intentions. Crystals associated with amplification and development, such as citrine and carnelian, may be charged under the waxing crescent's influence to enhance their vibrational potency.

As the moon progresses toward the first quarter, its illumination increases and the symbolic momentum intensifies. In ancient cultures, the first quarter moon was often linked to themes of action and overcoming obstacles. The Greeks, for example, associated the first quarter moon with the goddess Artemis, a symbol of strength, courage, and independence. The waxing moon's energy aligns with surmounting challenges and forging ahead on one's chosen path. This phase invites individuals to take proactive steps towards manifesting their intentions, embodying the spirit of progress and perseverance.

In Hindu mythology, the first quarter moon aligns with the waxing phase of Chandra, the lunar god. Chandra represents the pursuit of spiritual wisdom and virtue, making this phase conducive to endeavors that align with higher consciousness and personal development. The lunar cycle, infused with the symbolism of Chandra's journey, becomes a cosmic guide for those seeking growth in material pursuits and inner transformation.

In modern magical practices, the waxing crescent to the first quarter moon is often harnessed for intention-setting rituals that involve writing down goals, affirmations, or desires. During this phase, some practitioners create vision boards, visual representations of their aspirations. The intention is to focus on what is being actively cultivated and nurtured, aligning one's energies with the waxing moon's expansive influence.

The journey from the first quarter to the waxing gibbous moon marks a period of steady growth and fortification. In agricultural traditions, this phase corresponds to the maturation of crops, mirroring the idea of nurturing intentions into tangible fruition. The waxing gibbous phase invites individuals to assess the progress of their endeavors, make adjustments if necessary, and fortify their commitment to the goals set earlier in the lunar cycle.

In Chinese folklore, the waxing gibbous moon is associated with the moon goddess Chang'e and the Jade Rabbit. The story tells of Chang'e's ascent to the moon and the Jade Rabbit's ceaseless pounding of the elixir of immortality. The symbolism here includes themes of dedication, effort, and the steady pursuit of higher ideals. This cultural narrative resonates with the energies of the waxing gibbous moon, encouraging individuals to persist in their pursuits and invest effort into the growth process.

From a magical perspective, the waxing gibbous phase is conducive to spells and rituals that involve building, strengthening, and reinforcing intentions. This may include activities such as charging crystals for endurance and perseverance, crafting talismans to symbolize the growing energy of goals, or engaging in meditation practices aimed at consolidating focus and determination.

The lunar energy during this phase supports the incremental building of strength and resilience in the face of challenges.

Astrologically, the waxing gibbous moon often occurs in the zodiac sign opposing that of the sun. This opposition is considered a time of balance and integration, where the energies of the sun and moon work in tandem. Individuals may find that their lives external and internal aspects harmonize more effectively, creating a conducive environment for sustained growth and manifestation.

As the moon approaches full illumination, reaching the climax of its waxing phase, it enters the waxing gibbous stage to complete the moon transition. This is a pivotal period in the lunar cycle, often associated with peak energy, heightened intuition, and the culmination of intentions. With its radiant glow, the full moon serves as a beacon, symbolizing the manifestation of desires and the realization of goals.

Culturally, the full moon has been revered and celebrated across diverse traditions. In ancient Greece, the full moon was dedicated to the goddess Selene, embodying the moon's luminescent beauty and transformative power. The Romans similarly worshipped Luna during the full moon, recognizing its influence on the natural world and human emotions. Indigenous cultures often held ceremonies during the full moon, acknowledging its energetic potency and harnessing its illuminating power for communal and spiritual practices.

From a metaphysical standpoint, the full moon culminates the intentions set during the waxing crescent phase. Rituals during the full moon often involve charging crystals, tools, and personal items under its radiant light, infusing them with the heightened energy of manifestation. Some practitioners conduct esbat rituals, dedicated ceremonies during each full moon, to express gratitude, release stagnant energies, and celebrate the culmination of efforts.

Astrologically, the full moon opposes the sun and moon, representing a moment of illumination and clarity. This alignment is believed to heighten intuition, making it an auspicious time for divination, meditation, and reflection. A full moon's increased emotional energy may also bring unresolved feelings or concerns to the surface, allowing people to confront and let go of them.

The symbolism of the full moon is deeply ingrained in modern culture and folklore. Popular phrases like "once in a blue moon" or "over the moon" reflect the moon's influence on language and expressions. The concept of the full moon influencing human behavior, often called the "lunar effect," has been a subject of fascination and myth. While scientific studies have not conclusively proven a direct link between the full moon and changes in human behavior, the cultural impact of these beliefs persists.

In magical traditions, the full moon is often seen as a time for heightened magical workings, divination, and the culmination of spellcraft. Practitioners may conduct rituals to harness the full moon's energies for healing, manifestation, or spiritual empowerment. Water charged under the full moon, known as "moon water," is believed to carry potent lunar energy and is used in rituals, anointing, and spellwork.

During this phase, ceremonies frequently use full moon-related crystals like moonstone and selenite. Named for the moon goddess Selene, selenite is thought to improve spiritual awareness and communication with other dimensions. Moonstone, connected to lunar energy, is an effective tool for improving openness and intuition. Practitioners frequently place these crystals under the moon to purify and charge them and access their enhanced energies.

The full moon's influence extends into the realm of astrology, where each full moon occurs in a specific zodiac sign. The qualities and themes associated with that sign further flavor the energetic backdrop of the full moon. For example, a full moon in Aries may emphasize individuality, assertiveness, and initiation, while a full moon in Pisces may enhance sensitivity, intuition, and spiritual insights. Astrologers often guide, harnessing the unique energies of each full moon based on its zodiac placement.

In conclusion, the journey from the waxing crescent to the full moon in the lunar cycle is a symbolic expedition mirroring the manifestation and growth stages. Whether viewed through the lens of mythology, cultural practices, or magical traditions, the waxing moon's energy is one of progressive intention-setting, steady fortification, and eventual fruition. As the moon's glow intensifies, reaching its radiant fullness, individuals are invited to celebrate the culmination of their efforts, express gratitude, and bask in the transformative power of the lunar cycle. The waxing crescent to complete the moon phase serves as a cosmic reminder that the journey toward manifestation is not merely a linear progression but a rhythmic dance in harmony with the celestial forces that govern our existence.

Waning Gibbous to New Moon: Release and Renewal

The waning gibbous to the new moon phase in the lunar cycle represents a time of release, reflection, and renewal. As the moon transitions from its radiant fullness to the quiet darkness of the new moon, it carries with it the symbolism of shedding, letting go, and preparing for a new cycle of growth. This section explores the significance of the waning gibbous to the new moon phase, examining its cultural, spiritual, and metaphysical dimensions. Across various traditions and practices, this period is seen as an opportune moment for individuals to release what no longer serves them, engage in introspection, and set the stage for fresh beginnings.

Culturally, the waning gibbous to the new moon phase has been woven into the fabric of rituals and celebrations across different civilizations. In ancient Rome, the lunar goddess Luna, associated with the moon's cyclical changes, was also revered during the waning phases. The waning gibbous moon, slowly receding from its full illumination, marked a time for reflection on the passage of time, the ebb and flow of life, and the inevitable renewal. In Chinese culture, the waning moon is often linked to themes of closure and completion, aligning with the idea of concluding projects, releasing old patterns, and preparing for the new.

From a metaphysical perspective, the waning gibbous to the new moon phase is a potent time for letting go of energies and intentions that have come to fruition or are no longer aligned with one's path. In magical traditions, practitioners engage in banishing, releasing, and clearing rituals during this period. The waning gibbous moon's energy is harnessed to facilitate the removal of obstacles, negative energies, or unwanted influences. Spellwork during this phase may involve practices such as cord-cutting ceremonies, symbolic acts of releasing, or rituals that focus on breaking old patterns.

The waning gibbous moon is also associated with "waning" or decreasing energy. This energetic descent is seen as an opportunity to turn inward, reflecting on the experiences of the past lunar cycle and discerning what needs to be released. The diminishing moonlight corresponds with a gradual decrease in external energy, encouraging individuals to direct their focus inward for self-examination and introspection.

In astrology, the waning gibbous to new moon phase often occurs in the zodiac sign opposing that of the sun. This opposition creates a tension that can be channeled into the process of releasing and letting go. Individuals may find that external circumstances mirror internal processes during this phase, prompting them to address unresolved issues or emotional baggage.

In Hindu mythology, the waning crescent to the new moon phase aligns with the descent of Chandra, the lunar god, symbolizing the cyclical nature of life and death. This descent is not perceived as an ending but as a necessary step in the eternal dance of creation and dissolution. The waning crescent to the new moon phase is an invitation to release attachments, surrender what has served its purpose, and prepare for the next cycle of growth and evolution.

Waning moon rituals often involve practices of purification and energetic cleansing. It is customary to smudge with herbs like palo santo or sage because the smoke releases bottled-up energies and creates a sacred area for release. Crystals associated with letting go, such as obsidian and black tourmaline, may be used in rituals to absorb and transmute negative energies. These crystals are often buried in the earth or placed in running water to cleanse and recharge their energies for future use.

The waning gibbous to the new moon phase serves as a reminder that release is an integral part of the cyclical nature of existence. Just as the moon diminishes in brightness, so must individuals periodically shed what no longer serves their highest good. This process of intentional release aligns with the concept of "ego death" in spiritual traditions, where individuals surrender aspects of their identity that limit or hinder spiritual growth.

From a psychological standpoint, the waning gibbous to the new moon phase can be likened to a period of reflection and emotional detox. As the moon wanes, individuals may find it beneficial to engage in practices such as journaling, meditation, or therapy to explore and release emotions, thoughts, or patterns that are no longer beneficial. This internal reflection is crucial for personal growth and the cultivation of self-awareness.

In folk magic and traditional practices, the waning gibbous to new moon phase is a favorable time for banishing spells and rituals. This may involve writing down unwanted habits, situations, or energies on a piece of paper and burning or burying it as a symbolic act of release. Folk traditions often incorporate mirrors during this phase, believing that they can reflect and deflect negative energies away from the individual.

Astrologically, the waning gibbous to the new moon phase is associated with the closing of cycles and the preparation for new beginnings. It is a time to evaluate past actions, learn from experiences, and clear the slate for the next lunar cycle. The astrological sign in which the new moon occurs adds a nuanced flavor to this phase, influencing the themes of release and renewal based on the qualities of that particular sign.

In some Native American traditions, the waning gibbous to the new moon phase is linked to the concept of the "dark moon." This term refers to when the moon is not visible in the night sky. While some traditions differentiate between the dark moon and the new moon, both phases are often associated with introspection, dreaming, and tapping into the unseen realms. The dark moon is considered a time for going within, seeking guidance from the subconscious, and releasing attachments to the material world.

A sense of calm and stillness marks the transition from the waning gibbous to the new moon phase. The waning moon's diminishing light invites individuals to turn their attention inward, embrace the darkness, and find solace in the void. It is a time to release not only tangible aspects of life but also intangible ones, such as outdated beliefs, emotional burdens, or lingering resentments.

In conclusion, the waning gibbous to new moon phase in the lunar cycle is a powerful and transformative period associated with release and renewal. When considering things from the perspective of cultural customs, metaphysical practices, or psychological processes, this phase symbolizes the cyclical nature of life, inviting individuals to let go of what no longer serves them and make space for new growth. The intentional release during this period aligns with the universal rhythm of creation and dissolution, facilitating personal and spiritual evolution. As the moon enters the quiet darkness of the new moon, it carries with it the potential for rebirth, offering a blank canvas upon which new intentions can be sown in the cosmic dance of the lunar cycle.

CHAPTER III

Moonlit Tools and Altar Setup

Essential Tools for Moon Magic

Moon magic, a mystical practice rooted in ancient traditions and embraced by contemporary spiritual seekers, relies on various essential tools to amplify its potency and facilitate a deeper connection with lunar energies. These tools, ranging from symbolic representations to ritualistic instruments, serve as conduits for harnessing the ever-changing energies of the moon. In exploring essential tools for moon magic, we delve into the significance and usage of these instruments, understanding their roles in rituals, spellwork, and the cultivation of a profound relationship with the celestial luminary.

Crystals and gemstones are among moon magic's most revered and indispensable tools. Each crystal carries unique energetic properties, making them potent allies in aligning with specific lunar phases. Moonstone, named for its strong connection to the moon, is celebrated for enhancing intuition and receptivity. This ethereal stone is often utilized during the waxing crescent and complete moon phases, amplifying the energies of new beginnings and manifestation. Selenite, another crystal closely tied to the moon, is cherished for its purifying and high-vibrational properties. Practitioners use selenite to cleanse and charge other crystals, creating a harmonious and receptive energy field for moon magic.

The moon's influence extends beyond the night sky, shaping the ebb and flow of ocean tides. Water, as a symbolic representation of the moon's fluid nature, plays a pivotal role in moon magic rituals. Moonwater, water charged under the moon's light, is considered a versatile and potent tool. Practitioners collect moon water during specific lunar phases, harnessing the moon's energy to imbue the water with its transformative properties. Moonwater is then utilized for ritual purification, consecration of magical tools, and anointing during spells, creating a sacred link between the practitioner and the celestial forces at play.

Candles are essential tools in moon magic with their flickering flames and elemental connection to fire. Candle magic involves infusing candles with specific intentions and energies, aligning them with the lunar phases. During the waxing moon, candles often symbolize the growth of intentions and desires. With its peak energy, the full moon is a time for candles to represent the culmination of magical workings. Conversely, during the waning moon, candles become instruments for banishing rituals and releasing unwanted energies. The color of the candles further enhances their magical correspondences, with practitioners selecting hues that align with their intentions and the energy of the moon phase.

An altar, a sacred space dedicated to moon magic, is a focal point for rituals and spellwork. The arrangement of items on the altar is a personalized reflection of the practitioner's intentions and connection with the moon. Crystals, candles, moon water, and other tools are placed on the altar, creating a harmonious and energetically charged space. The altar is a physical manifestation of lunar energy and a symbolic link between the celestial powers called upon in moon magic rituals and the earthly plane.

Herbs and plants, revered for their magical properties and connection to the cycles of nature, are integral tools in moon magic. Each herb carries specific correspondences with lunar phases, adding depth and intention to rituals.

Mugwort, associated with the moon and dreams, is often used to enhance psychic abilities and visionary experiences during the waxing moon. With its calming and purifying qualities, Lavender finds a place on altars during the full moon for rituals of empowerment and manifestation. As the moon wanes, herbs like sage may be employed to purify and release rituals, release stale energy, and make room for fresh intentions.

With their reflective surfaces, mirrors hold a special place in moon magic as conduits for harnessing the moon's energies. Mirrors are often used in scrying, a divinatory practice involving gazing into reflective surfaces to receive insights and visions. During the full moon, when the moon's energy is believed to be at its peak, mirrors become portals for connecting with the intuitive and psychic realms. The mirror's reflective surface serves as a symbolic doorway, allowing practitioners to access more profound levels of consciousness and receive guidance from the unseen.

Tarot cards and other divination tools are significant in moon magic, offering insights and guidance aligned with the lunar energies. During the waxing moon, practitioners may engage in divination practices to clarify their intentions' unfolding potential. The full moon, a time of heightened intuition, is particularly auspicious for divination, as the veil between the seen and unseen realms is believed to thin. Tarot cards, oracle decks, and runes become channels through which practitioners receive messages from the intuitive realms, aiding in aligning actions with the moon's energies.

Inscriptions and symbols, often etched onto candles, crystals, or ritual tools, serve as encoded representations of intentions and energies in moon magic. Symbols like the crescent moon, representing new beginnings and potential, find prominence during the waxing moon phase. The full moon, a symbol of culmination and illumination, may be accompanied by symbols denoting empowerment and manifestation. During the waning moon, symbols of release and cleansing become focal points in rituals aimed at shedding unwanted energies. These inscriptions are potent reminders of the practitioner's intentions and provide a visual link between the physical tools and the metaphysical realms.

Anointing oils, infused with botanical essences and charged under the moon's light, are employed in moon magic to consecrate and amplify intentions. These oils, often crafted with herbs and crystals corresponding to specific lunar phases, carry the energetic imprints of the moon's influence. Anointing rituals, performed during different moon phases, involve applying oils, magical tools, or candles to the body. This act symbolizes invoking the moon's energy and aligning oneself with the moon's intentions during moon magic practices.

Moon phase calendars, a practical and informative tool, aid practitioners in planning and aligning their magical workings with the specific energies of each lunar phase. These calendars outline the dates and times of the new, waxing, complete, and waning moon, providing a roadmap for intentional rituals and spellwork. Moon phase calendars also incorporate astrological information, allowing practitioners to consider the additional influences of zodiac signs on the moon's energy during specific phases. This tool is a valuable resource for those seeking to deepen their connection with the moon's cycles and plan their magical workings accordingly.

In conclusion, essential tools for moon magic form a diverse and interconnected arsenal, each uniquely facilitating a profound connection with lunar energies. From crystals and candles to water and mirrors, these tools act as conduits, enhancing the potency of rituals and spellwork. The selection and use of these tools are highly personal, allowing practitioners to tailor their practices to align with their intentions and the specific energies of each moon phase. Whether drawing on ancient traditions or embracing contemporary adaptations, those who engage in moon magic find a rich tapestry of tools that amplify their connection with the celestial dance of the moon's cycles. As practitioners explore and integrate these tools into their magical repertoire, they unlock the transformative potential of moon magic, aligning their intentions with the ever-changing energies of the moonlit sky.

Creating a Sacred Space

Creating a sacred space is a transformative and deeply personal practice that transcends cultural, spiritual, and individual boundaries. It is a ritualized act of intentionally shaping and consecrating an environment to invite a sense of peace, connection, and divine presence. This section explores the multifaceted dimensions of creating a sacred space, delving into the significance, methods, and diverse cultural expressions encompassing this universal human endeavor.

Creating a sacred space is an ancient and cross-cultural practice deeply rooted in the human psyche. People and groups have tried to develop locations for rites, ceremonies, and times of spiritual connection throughout history. The concept of sacred space spans religious traditions, encompassing churches, temples, mosques, and shrines. Indigenous cultures, too, have their holy sites—natural landscapes, groves, or specific geographical features that hold profound spiritual significance. This universality underscores the human inclination to seek out or craft spaces that transcend the ordinary, providing a gateway to the transcendent.

The significance of a sacred space lies in its ability to serve as a sanctuary for the soul. In this haven, individuals can remove themselves from the clamor and expectations of the outside world. Whether within the confines of a designated room, a corner adorned with meaningful artifacts, or an outdoor setting embraced by nature, sacred spaces become vessels for contemplation, prayer, meditation, and spiritual rejuvenation. They are places where the mundane and the holy converge, offering individuals a tangible connection to the divine. However, they may conceive it.

In many spiritual traditions, creating a sacred space involves intentional purification and consecration. Rituals, prayers, and symbolic gestures transform ordinary spaces into realms charged with spiritual energy. In Christianity, consecrating a church involves invoking divine blessings, anointing with sacred oils, and conducting rituals to set the space apart for holy practices. Similarly, in Hinduism, the consecration of a temple is a meticulously choreographed ceremony involving intricate rituals and the infusion of divine energy into the temple's sanctum. These practices underline the belief that the physical space can become a vessel for the sacred, as a bridge between the material and spiritual realms.

Individuals who engage in personal or eclectic spiritual practices also embrace creating a sacred space within their homes or chosen environments. The process often involves selecting meaningful objects, such as candles, crystals, religious icons, or personal artifacts arranged with intentionality. The placement of these items is not arbitrary; instead, it reflects the practitioner's unique spiritual path, connecting them with symbols and energies that resonate with their beliefs and aspirations. The consecration may involve prayers, invocations, or a focused mindset that imbues the space with reverence.

With its inherent beauty and transformative power, nature serves as a sacred space for many individuals. Whether it be a secluded grove, a mountain peak, a flowing river, or a serene meadow, the outdoors offers a canvas for creating sacred spaces untethered by walls or artificial structures. Indigenous cultures worldwide have long recognized the sanctity of natural landscapes, considering their portals to the divine. The intentional act of communing with nature through meditation, ceremony, or solitary reflection can transform a chosen spot into a sacred space that fosters a deep connection with the earth and the cosmos.

The methods employed in creating a sacred space are as diverse as the cultures and belief systems that engage in this practice. One common thread, however, is the intentional and mindful approach to arranging and consecrating the space. The process often begins with clearing the space of clutter and discordant energies. This can be achieved through physical cleaning, smudging with holy plants such as palo santo or sage, or using sound, such as bells or singing bowls, to dispel stagnant energies. The cleansing symbolizes preparing the canvas to infuse positive and sacred energies.

The selection and arrangement of meaningful objects are pivotal in creating a sacred space. These objects, often called altar items, may include religious symbols, candles, crystals, sculptures, and personal mementos. The arrangement is guided by the practitioner's spiritual inclinations and the energy they wish to cultivate within the space. For example, a meditation altar may feature items that promote serenity and introspection, while an altar dedicated to rituals may include tools associated with the practitioner's specific tradition.

Natural and artificial lighting are crucial elements in establishing the ambiance of a sacred space. Candles, with their flickering flames, are widely used to represent illumination and spiritual presence. The color and scent of the candles may be chosen based on their correspondence with specific intentions or energies. Natural light, if available, is often considered auspicious and is utilized to enhance the vibrancy of the space.

Windows may be adorned with sheer fabrics or crystals to refract and diffuse sunlight, creating a serene and ethereal atmosphere.

The use of sacred geometry and patterns contributes to the energetic alignment of a holy space. Mandalas, labyrinth designs, or specific arrangements of objects may be incorporated to evoke a sense of harmony and balance. These geometric patterns are believed to resonate with universal energies and archetypal symbols, serving as conduits for the practitioner to attune to higher states of consciousness. The deliberate use of geometry aligns with the belief that specific shapes and patterns carry inherent vibrational frequencies that can enhance the spiritual atmosphere of a space.

Soundscapes, including chants, mantras, music, or the soothing sounds of nature, contribute to the auditory ambiance of a sacred space. Sound can evoke specific emotions, alter consciousness, and create a receptive state for spiritual practices. Bells, singing bowls, or wind chimes are often employed for their ability to produce resonant tones that clear stagnant energies and attune the space to higher frequencies. The auditory component of a sacred space adds a dynamic layer to the overall experience, engaging multiple senses in spiritual attunement.

Intuition and personal resonance guide the selection of colors in a sacred space. Different hues carry unique energetic qualities and correspondences, influencing the overall atmosphere of the space. Warm tones like red and orange may be incorporated for vitality and passion, while cool tones like blue and green evoke tranquility and healing. The practitioner's cultural background, spiritual tradition, and personal preferences all play a role in determining the color palette of their sacred space. The intentional use of colors aligns with the understanding that visual stimuli can profoundly impact a space's energetic and emotional dynamics.

Sacred texts, scriptures, or written affirmations are often included in creating a holy space. These written elements anchor the practitioner's intentions, providing a tangible link to sacred teachings or personal affirmations. Whether it be a religious scripture, a book of poetry, or handwritten affirmations, the presence of written words reinforces the sacredness of the space. It acts as a focal point for meditation and reflection.

The sacred space is not static but a dynamic and evolving reflection of the practitioner's spiritual journey. Regular care and upkeep are vital to guarantee that the area stays energetically attuned and supportive of spiritual practices. This may involve periodic cleansing rituals, rearranging altar items based on evolving intentions, or introducing new elements that resonate with the practitioner's spiritual growth. The intentional engagement with the sacred space fosters an ongoing relationship, where the space becomes a living expression of the practitioner's inner landscape.

In conclusion, creating a sacred space is a profound and universal practice that transcends cultural, religious, and individual boundaries. It is an intentional and transformative act that allows individuals to connect with the sacred through established religious traditions, personal spiritual practices, or communion with nature. The methods employed in creating a holy space are diverse, reflecting the unique perspectives and intentions of the practitioners. From the clearing of energies to the arrangement of meaningful objects, from the use of symbolism to the incorporation of sound and light, each element contributes to the overall tapestry of a space that invites transcendence, contemplation, and connection with the divine. As individuals continue to explore and adapt this practice, creating sacred spaces becomes a timeless and evolving journey—a testament to the enduring human quest for the holy in the midst of the ordinary.

Altar Decor and Symbolism

Altar decor and symbolism are integral to spiritual and magical practices across diverse cultures and belief systems. An altar, a sacred space designated for ritualistic and ceremonial activities, is a focal point for practitioners to connect with the divine, set intentions, and engage in transformative energies. The items chosen to adorn an altar are carefully selected based on their symbolic significance, aligning with the practitioner's spiritual path, intentions, and the energies of the specific rituals. This section explores the rich tapestry of altar decor and symbolism, delving into how individuals craft meaningful and potent sacred spaces.

At the heart of altar decor and symbolism lies the intention to create a space with spiritual energy and resonance. Each item on the altar serves as a conduit for the practitioner to connect with specific energies, deities, or spiritual principles. R revered for their unique energetic properties; Crystals find a prominent place on many altars. From hematite's grounding energy to amethyst's intuitive insights, crystals are selected based on their correspondences with the practitioner's intentions and the moon's phases or other celestial cycles.

Candles, with their flickering flames, are ubiquitous in altar decor across various spiritual traditions. The symbolism of fire represents transformation, illumination, and the sacred flame that connects the earthly realm with the divine. The color of the candles further contributes to the symbolism, with each hue resonating with specific intentions and energies. For example, a red candle may symbolize passion and vitality, while a blue candle may represent tranquility and spiritual communication.

Statuary and images of deities or spiritual figures play a central role in altar decor, embodying the divine qualities and archetypal energies associated with these beings. In Hinduism, altars often feature statues of gods and goddesses such as Ganesha for removing obstacles or Lakshmi for abundance. Similarly, in Wiccan traditions, altars may include representations of the Horned God and the Triple Goddess. These figures are focal points for devotion, meditation, and invoking specific qualities or blessings.

Sacred symbols, imbued with esoteric meaning, find a place on altars as potent tools for transformation and connection. The pentacle, an ancient symbol of protection and the elements is commonly used in Wiccan and pagan traditions. The om symbol, resonating with the vibration of the universe, is revered in Hinduism and other Eastern spiritual paths. These symbols act as gateways, aligning the practitioner with higher realms and providing a visual language for expressing spiritual concepts.

Herbs and botanicals, often dried or arranged in bundles, contribute to altar decor and bring the energies of the natural world into the sacred space. Sage bundles, used for smudging and purification, are prevalent in many indigenous and contemporary spiritual practices. Lavender, associated with healing and tranquility, may find its place on altars dedicated to meditation and serenity. Herbs connect the practitioner with the earth's energies and add a sensory dimension to the altar space.

Ancestral altars, honoring departed loved ones and ancestors, are adorned with items that symbolize connection and remembrance. Photographs, mementos, and personal belongings of the ancestors serve as tangible links to the past. Offerings such as food, drink, or symbolic items are placed on the ancestral altar to nourish and honor the spirits of those who have passed on. The symbolism in ancestral altars is deeply personal, reflecting the unique relationships and legacies of the practitioner's familial lineage.

With their distinct energies and symbolism, the moon's phases influence altar decor in practices like moon magic and witchcraft. During the waxing moon, when energy is building, and intentions are gaining momentum, altars may feature symbols of growth, such as blooming flowers or representations of the crescent moon. The full moon, a time of culmination and illumination, inspires altars adorned with items symbolizing manifestation and peak energy. Conversely, the waning moon calls for altar decor that aligns with releasing and letting go, incorporating symbols of completion and closure.

Astrological symbols, corresponding to the positions of celestial bodies at specific times, add a layer of complexity to altar decor and symbolism. Practitioners who work with astrology may include symbols of their zodiac sign, planetary symbols, or other astrological correspondences on their altars. This cosmic language enhances the practitioner's ability to attune to the energetic influences of celestial bodies and astrological events.

Altar cloths, chosen for their color, texture, and symbolism, form the foundation of altar decor. The fabric's color often aligns with the practitioner's intentions and the energies they wish to invoke. In many traditions, specific colors carry symbolic meanings; for example, green may symbolize prosperity, while white represents purity and spiritual illumination. The texture of the cloth adds a tactile dimension to the altar, influencing the overall sensory experience of the sacred space.

Tarot cards, oracle decks, or runes may find a place on altars as tools for divination and spiritual guidance. The practitioner may draw cards or cast runes to receive insights, messages, or clarity on their spiritual journey. Including divination tools on the altar emphasizes the practitioner's commitment to seeking guidance from higher realms and aligning with intuitive wisdom.

Bells, chimes, or other sound instruments contribute to altar decor by adding an auditory element to the sacred space. The sound produced by these instruments serves as a means of clearing stagnant energies, marking transitions between ritual phases, or invoking spiritual beings. The intentional use of sound enhances the vibrational frequency of the altar, creating a dynamic and resonant environment.

Sacred texts, scriptures, or books that hold spiritual significance are often placed on altars as sources of wisdom and inspiration. These texts may include religious scriptures, grimoires, poetry, or philosophical writings. The presence of sacred texts serves as a reminder of the practitioner's spiritual principles and provides a tangible link to the teachings that guide their path.

Personal items, charged with sentimental or emotional value, find a place on altars to infuse the sacred space with the practitioner's unique energy. These may include photographs, heirlooms, or symbolic objects that hold personal significance. Having personal items adds a layer of intimacy to the altar, creating a space that is spiritually charged and deeply connected to the practitioner's journey.

The placement and arrangement of items on an altar are not arbitrary; instead, they are guided by the principles of sacred geometry and energetic alignment. Practitioners often arrange items to create balance, symmetry, and a harmonious flow of energy. The intentional placement of items on the altar reflects the practitioner's understanding of energy dynamics and their ability to attune the space to higher frequencies.

In conclusion, altar decor and symbolism form a rich, intricate tapestry in spiritual and magical practices. Altars serve as portals to the divine, allowing practitioners to engage with transformative energies, set intentions, and cultivate a deeper connection with the sacred. The items chosen for altar decor are imbued with symbolic significance, representing archetypal energies, cultural traditions, and personal intentions. Whether adorned with crystals, candles, statuary, symbols, or personal items, altars become living expressions of the practitioner's spiritual journey, evolving and resonating with the ever- changing currents of their inner landscape. As individuals continue to explore and adapt the practice of altar decor and symbolism, they unlock the potential for profound spiritual experiences, tapping into the timeless wisdom that transcends cultural and individual boundaries.

CHAPTER IV

Lunar Correspondences

Moon in Zodiac Signs

The Moon's journey through the twelve zodiac signs is a celestial dance that influences the ebb and flow of emotions, instincts, and inner energies. The Moon, the nearest heavenly body to Earth, profoundly affects human psychology. It is said that an individual's emotional inclinations, subconscious patterns, and reactions are shaped by their birth chart's placement in the zodiac. The Moon symbolizes the inner self, the changing environment, and the innate responses that direct our actions in astrology. Every sign in the zodiac distinctly imbues the Moon, influencing the emotional background of a person's personality. This section illuminates the colorful tapestry that this celestial luminary weaves by examining the subtle manifestations of the Moon in each zodiac sign.

Aries, the first sign of the zodiac, infuses the Moon with fiery and assertive energy. A passionate and impulsive approach to emotions characterizes those with the Moon in Aries. Their feelings are dynamic and vibrant, often expressed with enthusiasm and spontaneity. The Aries Moon imbues individuals with a sense of independence and a desire for emotional autonomy. However, challenges may arise when impatience or impulsivity takes precedence, leading to sudden emotional flare-ups. Nurturing the Aries Moon involves allowing space for self-expression, encouraging healthy outlets for passion, and fostering a balance between independence and collaboration.

Taurus, an earth sign ruled by Venus, bestows the Moon with stability, sensuality, and a grounding influence. A need for security and comfort often characterizes individuals with the Moon in Taurus. Taurus Moons find solace in routines, material comforts, and the beauty of nature. While their emotional landscape is generally calm, challenges may arise if they become too attached to the familiar or resistant to change. Nurturing the Taurus Moon involves creating a stable and aesthetically pleasing environment, engaging in sensory experiences, and cultivating flexibility in the face of change.

Gemini, an air sign ruled by Mercury, imparts the Moon with intellectual curiosity, adaptability, and a need for mental stimulation. Those with the Moon in Gemini are characterized by a quicksilver emotional nature, where feelings are processed through the lens of the mind. Communication is a crucial aspect of emotional expression for Gemini Moons, who may find comfort in verbalizing their emotions or engaging in diverse social interactions. Challenges may arise when the mind becomes overwhelmed, leading to restlessness or emotional detachment. Nurturing the Gemini Moon involves fostering intellectual pursuits, encouraging open communication, and providing outlets for mental stimulation.

Cancer, the Moon's ruling sign, brings a profound emotional depth and nurturing quality to the lunar landscape. Individuals with the Moon in Cancer are highly attuned to their emotions and possess a strong instinct for caretaking. Family and home play a central role in their emotional fulfillment, and there is a natural inclination to create a secure and nurturing environment. While the Cancer Moon is empathetic and compassionate, challenges may arise when emotional sensitivity becomes overwhelming or when there is resistance to change. Nurturing the Cancer Moon involves honoring emotional needs, creating a supportive home environment, and developing healthy boundaries.

Leo, the Sun-ruled fire sign, enhances the Moon's power with a dash of drama, originality, and self-expression. Those with the Moon in Leo are characterized by a need for recognition, admiration, and the freedom to express their authentic selves. Emotions are experienced with a theatrical flair, and there is a desire to be seen and appreciated. Challenges may arise when the need for validation becomes excessive, or pride interferes with vulnerability. Nurturing the Leo Moon involves celebrating individuality, encouraging creative expression, and fostering a sense of self-worth independent of external validation.

Virgo, an earth sign ruled by Mercury, instills the Moon with practicality, analytical skills, and a penchant for organization. Individuals with the Moon in Virgo are characterized by a need for order, efficiency, and a desire to serve. Emotions are processed through a lens of discernment, and there is a practical approach to nurturing and caretaking. Challenges may arise when the pursuit of perfection becomes a source of anxiety or overthinking. Nurturing the Virgo Moon involves creating organized and harmonious environments, engaging in practical self-care, and cultivating self-compassion.

Libra, an air sign ruled by Venus, adds a sense of harmony, diplomacy, and a yearning for connection to the Moon's influence. A need for balance, beauty, and harmonious relationships characterizes those with the Moon in Libra. Emotions are often experienced about others, and there is a desire for fairness and cooperation. Challenges may arise when the quest for harmony leads to avoidance of conflict or when there is a tendency to prioritize others' needs over one's own. Nurturing the Libra Moon involves cultivating balance in relationships, creating aesthetically pleasing environments, and developing assertiveness.

Scorpio, a water sign ruled by Pluto, brings intensity, depth, and transformative qualities to the Moon's influence. A profound emotional depth, a desire for authenticity, and an innate understanding of the hidden realms of emotion characterize individuals with the Moon in Scorpio. Emotions are experienced with intensity, and there is a need for profound connection and intimacy. Challenges may arise when emotional intensity leads to power struggles or resistance to vulnerability. Nurturing the Scorpio Moon involves embracing emotional authenticity, fostering deep connections, and engaging in transformative practices.

Sagittarius, a fire sign ruled by Jupiter, imparts the Moon with adventurous, optimistic, and expansive qualities. A need for freedom, exploration, and a philosophical approach to emotions characterizes those with the Moon in Sagittarius. Emotions are experienced with enthusiasm, and there is a desire for growth and expansion. Challenges may arise when restlessness interferes with emotional depth or when there is a tendency to avoid emotional intimacy. Nurturing the Sagittarius Moon involves encouraging exploration, embracing a sense of humor, and fostering a connection to higher truths.

Capricorn, an earth sign ruled by Saturn, adds a sense of discipline, responsibility, and ambition to the Moon's influence. Individuals with the Moon in Capricorn are characterized by a need for structure, achievement, and a desire for mastery over emotions. Emotions are often approached with a sense of practicality, and there is a natural inclination to take on responsibilities. Challenges may arise when the pursuit of success becomes a source of emotional detachment or when there is a fear of vulnerability. Nurturing the Capricorn Moon involves creating achievable goals, establishing healthy boundaries, and balancing work and emotional well- being.

Aquarius, an air sign ruled by Uranus, instills the Moon with innovation, independence, and a desire for collective progress. A need for individuality, intellectual stimulation, and a sense of social purpose characterizes those with the Moon in Aquarius. Emotions are often experienced with a detached and objective perspective, and there is a desire to contribute to the greater good. Challenges may arise when emotional detachment interferes with personal relationships or when there is resistance to vulnerability. Nurturing the Aquarius Moon involves embracing uniqueness, fostering community, and engaging in progressive and humanitarian pursuits.

A deep emotional sensitivity, a rich inner world, and a desire for transcendence characterize individuals with the Moon in Pisces. Emotions are experienced with empathy and a fluid, imaginative quality. Challenges may arise when emotional boundaries become blurred or when there is a tendency to escape into fantasy. Nurturing the Pisces Moon involves cultivating creativity, embracing intuitive insights, and creating a sacred space for emotional expression.

In conclusion, the Moon's journey through the zodiac signs intricately weaves a tapestry of emotional nuances, coloring the inner landscape of individuals with its celestial influence. Each placement offers a unique blend of qualities, instincts, and tendencies that shape how emotions are experienced and expressed. Understanding the Moon's position in the natal chart provides valuable insights into one's emotional needs and reactions and how the inner self seeks fulfillment and connection with the more extensive cosmic dance. As individuals explore the depth and richness of their Moon sign, they uncover a profound aspect of their astrological identity, unlocking the door to a deeper understanding of the self and the emotional currents that shape their journey through life.

Moon in Astrological Houses

The Moon's placement in the astrological houses is critical in understanding the nuanced interplay between emotions, instincts, and the various areas of life. As one of the most influential luminaries in astrology, the Moon symbolizes our inner self, emotional responses, and subconscious patterns that shape our experiences. The twelve astrological houses represent different facets of life, each influencing specific areas such as relationships, career, home, and personal identity. When the Moon is situated in a particular house at the time of one's birth, it colors the emotional landscape. It shapes the individual's approach to the themes associated with that house. This section explores the diverse expressions of the Moon in each astrological house, shedding light on how lunar influences manifest within the context of various life domains.

The Moon in the first house, often associated with the self and identity, imbues individuals with a strong emotional presence. These individuals are deeply attuned to their inner world, and emotions are readily visible in their demeanor. The first house Moon suggests a person who is instinctively responsive to the environment and possesses a keen self-awareness. This placement may enhance emotional expressiveness, making these individuals open and approachable. However, challenges may arise if there is a tendency to be overly reactive or emotional fluctuations impact the sense of self. Nurturing the Moon in the first house involves cultivating a healthy self-image, embracing emotional authenticity, and developing a balanced approach to self-expression.

When the Moon graces the second house, associated with values, resources, and self-worth, emotional fulfillment is often intertwined with material security. Individuals with the Moon in the second house may find comfort and emotional stability in a secure and stable financial environment. There is a deep connection between emotions and the material world; these individuals may derive a sense of self-worth from their possessions. Challenges may arise if there is an overemphasis on earthly security as a source of emotional well-being or a fear of financial instability. Nurturing the Moon in the second house involves finding emotional fulfillment through a balanced approach to material and emotional needs, cultivating self-worth independent of possessions, and developing a healthy relationship with money.

The Moon in the third house, associated with communication, learning, and siblings, suggests a strong emotional connection to ideas and information. These individuals may have a deep need for intellectual stimulation and emotional fulfillment through communication. There is a natural curiosity and receptivity to new ideas, and emotions may find expression through verbal or written means. Challenges may arise if there is a tendency to become overly analytical or if emotions are suppressed in favor of rationality. Nurturing the Moon in the third house involves fostering open and honest communication, engaging in continuous learning, and finding emotional fulfillment through intellectual pursuits.

Emotions find their most profound expression in the fourth house, the natural home of the Moon in the astrological chart. This placement is associated with the roots, home, family, and the nurturing environment. Individuals with the Moon in the fourth house are deeply connected to their familial and ancestral heritage, and emotional fulfillment is often sought through a sense of belonging and security in the home. There is a strong desire for a stable and nurturing family life, and these individuals may find solace in creating a harmonious home environment. Challenges may arise if resistance to change or emotional security is tied to the past. Nurturing the Moon in the fourth house involves creating a supportive home environment, connecting with family roots, and embracing emotional vulnerability.

When the Moon graces the fifth house, associated with creativity, self-expression, and romance, emotions find an outlet through creative pursuits and personal passions. A vibrant and expressive emotional nature characterizes individuals with the Moon in the fifth house. There is a desire for playful self-expression, and emotions may be channeled into artistic endeavors or romantic relationships. These individuals may seek emotional fulfillment through activities that bring joy and self-expression. Challenges arise if there is a tendency to seek validation through external sources or if emotions become overly dramatic. Nurturing the Moon in the fifth house involves embracing creative outlets, fostering a sense of playfulness, and finding emotional fulfillment through self-expression.

In the sixth house, associated with work, health, and daily routines, the Moon influences emotional well-being through service and practical activities. Individuals with the Moon in the sixth house may find emotional fulfillment in a structured and organized approach to daily life. A nurturing quality is expressed through acts of service and a desire for a healthy and harmonious work environment. Challenges may arise if there is an excessive focus on perfectionism or emotions are suppressed in favor of routine tasks. Nurturing the Moon in the sixth house involves cultivating a balanced and healthy daily routine, finding emotional satisfaction through acts of service, and addressing emotional needs in work and health.

When the Moon occupies the seventh house, associated with partnerships, relationships, and one-on-one connections, emotions are intimately tied to interpersonal dynamics. Individuals with the Moon in the seventh house seek emotional fulfillment through close relationships and partnerships. There is a strong desire for harmony, emotional connection, and mutual understanding in relationships. Challenges may arise if a fear of emotional vulnerability or dependency on others for emotional fulfillment becomes excessive. Nurturing the Moon in the seventh house involves fostering healthy and balanced relationships, developing emotional authenticity in partnerships, and recognizing the interdependence of emotions within the context of relationships.

In the eighth house, associated with transformation, shared resources, and intimate connections, the Moon delves into the depths of emotional intensity. Individuals with the Moon in the eighth house may experience profound and complex emotions. There is a natural inclination towards emotional transformation and a desire for intense and intimate connections. Emotional fulfillment may be sought through shared experiences and a deep understanding of the mysteries of life. Challenges may arise if a fear of vulnerability or emotional intensity leads to power struggles. Nurturing the Moon in the eighth house involves embracing emotional depth, cultivating intimacy in relationships, and navigating the transformative aspects of emotions.

The Moon in the ninth house, associated with higher learning, philosophy, and travel, suggests a connection between emotions and a quest for knowledge and understanding. Individuals with the Moon in the ninth house may find emotional fulfillment through exploration, learning, and a broadened perspective. There is a desire for meaning and purpose, and emotions may be expressed through philosophical or spiritual pursuits. Challenges may arise if one avoids emotional depth in favor of intellectual pursuits or resistance to exploring new perspectives. Nurturing the Moon in the ninth house involves integrating emotions with a quest for higher knowledge, embracing diverse belief systems, and finding emotional fulfillment through expansive experiences.

When the Moon graces the tenth house, associated with career, public life, and achievements, emotions are closely tied to one's professional identity and public image. Individuals with the Moon in the tenth house may find emotional fulfillment through career success, public recognition, and a sense of accomplishment. There is a desire for emotional security in the public sphere, and the nurturing qualities may be expressed through a professional role. Challenges may arise if there is an overemphasis on external validation or emotions are suppressed in pursuing career goals. Nurturing the Moon in the tenth house involves aligning professional endeavors with emotional fulfillment, balancing public and private life, and recognizing the impact of emotions on career aspirations.

In the eleventh house, associated with the community, social connections, and aspirations, the Moon influences emotions through a sense of belonging to a larger collective. Individuals with the Moon in the eleventh house may find emotional fulfillment through social connections, group activities, and shared ideals. There is a desire for a sense of community and emotional support from like-minded individuals. Challenges may arise if there is a fear of emotional vulnerability in group settings or emotional needs are neglected in pursuing collective goals. Nurturing the Moon in the eleventh house involves fostering a sense of community, embracing shared aspirations, and recognizing the importance of emotional connections within social circles.

When the Moon occupies the twelfth house, associated with the subconscious, spirituality, and the collective unconscious, emotions find expression in the psyche's hidden realms. Individuals with the Moon in the twelfth house may experience deep spiritual and subconscious emotions. A desire for emotional transcendence is expressed through spiritual practices, dreams, or a connection to the collective unconscious. Challenges may arise if one represses emotions or emotional experiences become overwhelming. Nurturing the Moon in the twelfth house involves exploring the depths of the subconscious, engaging in spiritual practices, and finding emotional release through creative and reflective outlets.

In conclusion, the Moon's placement in the astrological houses adds depth and complexity to understanding emotional influences in various areas of life. Each house represents a distinct life domain, and the Moon's position shapes the dynamic landscape within those domains. Understanding the interplay between the Moon and the astrological houses provides valuable insights into how individuals seek emotional fulfillment, navigate challenges, and express their innermost selves within the diverse tapestry of life experiences. As individuals explore the nuances of their Moon's placement, they uncover a profound aspect of their astrological identity, unlocking the door to a deeper understanding of the self and the emotional currents that shape their journey through the intricacies of existence.

Aligning Spells with Lunar Phases

Aligning spells with lunar phases is a profound and time-honored practice that taps into the cyclical energies of the moon, harnessing its influence to enhance the potency of magical workings. The moon has captured people's attention with its ever-changing phases for millennia, acting as a heavenly guide for various mystical and spiritual endeavors. The moon is seen as a potent ally in spellcraft, and practitioners frequently time their rituals to coincide with particular lunar phases to synchronize their magic with the universe's inherent cycles.

The lunar cycle consists of eight distinct phases, each holding unique energetic qualities and symbolic significance. The New Moon marks the beginning of the cycle, representing a time of new beginnings, intention setting, and planting seeds for future growth. As the moon waxes, moving from the Waxing Crescent to the First Quarter, the energy intensifies, supporting manifestation, development, and the amplification of intentions. This phase is ideal for spells involving building, attracting, and setting plans.

The Full Moon, which occurs halfway through the lunar cycle, is decisive for the climax and pinnacle of magical operations. It symbolizes abundance, illumination, and the fulfillment of desires. Spells cast during the Full Moon often focus on manifestation, heightened intuition, and harnessing the maximum lunar energy. Following the Full Moon, the waning phases—Waning Gibbous, Third Quarter, and Waning Crescent—mark a period of release, reflection, and banishing. These phases are conducive to spells aimed at letting go, shedding unwanted energies, and clearing obstacles.

One of the critical principles in aligning spells with lunar phases is recognizing the moon's influence on the ebb and flow of energy. The moon's gravitational pull affects Earth's tides, and just as it influences the vast oceans, it is believed to influence the subtle energies that flow through all living things. Practitioners of lunar magic harness this gravitational pull, syncing their intentions with the corresponding energy of each lunar phase to amplify the effectiveness of their spells.

The energy is favorable for new beginnings and fresh begins during the New Moon when the moon is in conjunction with the Sun and unseen from Earth. During this stage, spells are frequently used to start undertakings, sow seeds of intention, and provide the foundation for development. The New Moon's blackness represents the void that is fruitful and gives rise to possibilities. To match their energies with the possibility of new manifestations, practitioners can participate in rituals like visualization, meditation, or candle magic.

Moving into the Waxing Crescent phase, the first sliver of the moon becomes visible, symbolizing the emergence of intention into the material realm. This phase is ideal for spells focused on growth, expansion, and attracting positive influences. Spells may involve visualization techniques, the charging of crystals or talismans, and the crafting of affirmations to support the intentions set during the New Moon. The energy intensifies as the moon waxes towards the first quarter, propelling intentions forward and helping build momentum.

The First Quarter, halfway between the New Moon and the Full Moon, is a time of action and overcoming obstacles. The energy is dynamic, and spells during this phase are often geared toward removing barriers, making decisions, and taking decisive steps toward goals. Rituals may involve using correspondences such as herbs, colors, and symbols that align with the practitioner's intentions and the qualities associated with the First Quarter moon, such as courage and determination.

The Full Moon, standing at the pinnacle of the lunar cycle, bathes the world in its luminous glow. This phase is a pivotal point for spellwork, offering a powerful surge of energy for manifestation, divination, and heightened intuition. Spells cast during the Full Moon may include rituals for abundance, love, and spiritual insight. The Full Moon's radiant energy is harnessed by charging crystals and consecrating tools, and ceremonies are performed under its ethereal light.

As the moon transitions into the Waning Gibbous phase, it begins to wane, signaling a time for reflection, assessment, and release. This phase is apt for spells aimed at banishing negativity, breaking unhealthy habits, and letting go of what no longer serves. Practitioners may engage in rituals that involve cleansing, purifying, and releasing energy, allowing the waning moon to support the process of shedding unwanted influences.

The Third Quarter, marking the moon's journey to the last quarter before the New Moon signifies a time for resolution and closure. Spells during this phase may focus on completing projects, resolving conflicts, and tying up loose ends. The energy is still waning, supporting the release process and making space for new intentions. Rituals may involve symbolic closure actions, such as burning written releases or engaging in meditative practices to bring a sense of resolution.

This phase is a potent time for deep introspection, spiritual cleansing, and preparing for the upcoming New Moon. Spells during this phase may involve divination, dreamwork, and connecting with the subconscious mind. Practitioners may perform rituals facilitating inner healing, intuition development, and spiritual guidance. Aligning spells with lunar phases requires understanding the specific energies associated with each phase and a deliberate attunement of magical workings to those energies. The waxing phases are characterized by building and amplifying energy, making them suitable for growth, attraction, and manifestation spells. Conversely, the waning phases are associated with releasing, banishing, and clearing energies, making them conducive to spells aimed at letting go, breaking habits, and removing obstacles.

Practitioners often use correspondences, such as colors, herbs, crystals, and symbols, to align their intentions with the moon's energy. For example, green may be chosen for spells related to growth and abundance, while black may be selected for banishing and releasing rituals. Crystals like moonstone, clear quartz, or obsidian may be incorporated to amplify the energetic resonance of the spell. These correspondences serve as symbolic tools that enhance the practitioner's connection to the specific qualities of each lunar phase.

Moon magic also emphasizes the importance of ritual and ceremony in spellwork. Practitioners may create elaborate rituals or simple ceremonies, depending on the intensity and focus required for their intentions. Rituals may include meditation, visualization, candle magic, and the use of magical tools to amplify the energy and symbolism of the spell. Engaging the senses, such as incorporating aromas, sounds, and tactile experiences, adds depth to the ritual and enhances the practitioner's connection to the lunar energies.

The moon's influence on water is a significant aspect of lunar magic, and many practitioners incorporate water in their spellwork. Water is believed to be a conduit for lunar energy, and spells involving consecration, purification, and manifestation often include using moon-charged water. This may involve placing water under the moonlight to absorb its energies, creating moon water, and using it as a sacred tool in spellcasting.

Astrological considerations also play a role in aligning spells with lunar phases. The moon moves through each zodiac sign approximately every two to three days, imbuing the lunar energies with the qualities associated with each sign. Practitioners may choose specific times during the lunar cycle when the moon is in a particular zodiac sign to enhance the resonance of their spells. For example, casting a love spell during a Full Moon in Libra, ruled by Venus, may amplify the energies associated with love, harmony, and partnership.

In conclusion, aligning spells with lunar phases is a profoundly symbolic and practical practice that harmonizes the practitioner's intentions with the cyclical energies of the moon. The eight lunar cycle phases provide a roadmap for spellwork, guiding practitioners through setting intentions, manifesting desires, releasing obstacles, and culminating in a renewal cycle. By understanding the energetic qualities of each lunar phase, incorporating correspondences, and engaging in ritualistic practices, practitioners of lunar magic tap into the primal forces of the cosmos, weaving their intentions into the intricate dance of the moonlit sky. Whether working with the waxing crescent, the full moon, or the waning crescent, aligning spells with lunar phases offers a profound connection to the natural rhythms of the universe, unlocking the potential for transformative and magical experiences in the realm of spellcraft.

CHAPTER V

Moonlit Spells for Everyday Magic

Love and Relationships

Love and relationships constitute a fundamental aspect of the human experience, shaping the tapestry of our lives with emotional richness, joy, and profound connections. From the early stages of infatuation to the complexities of long-term commitment, the journey of love encompasses a spectrum of emotions, challenges, and transformative experiences. Understanding the dynamics of love and relationships involves delving into the intricacies of human connection and exploring the psychological, emotional, and social factors contributing to romantic partnerships' formation, maintenance, and evolution.

The foundations of love often find their roots in attraction—a magnetic force that draws individuals together in a dance of discovery. Fueled by genetic, hormonal, and cultural factors, physical attraction sets the stage for the initial spark that ignites romantic interest. As individuals navigate the attraction landscape, psychological factors such as personality compatibility, shared values, and everyday interests are pivotal in deepening the connection. The process of falling in love is a complex interplay of conscious choices, subconscious desires, and the mysterious alchemy of chemistry.

The early stages of a romantic relationship are characterized by infatuation, a state marked by heightened emotions, intense focus on the object of affection, and a sense of euphoria. This infatuation phase, often called the "honeymoon period," is a time of exploration and joy where couples revel in the novelty of their connection. However, as the initial surge of infatuation begins to settle, couples enter a phase of reality testing. This stage is marked by a deeper exploration of each other's personalities, values, and quirks, providing a more nuanced understanding of compatibility and potential challenges.

This stage is when communication, essential to happy relationships, becomes even more critical. In addition to expressing ideas and emotions, effective communication requires empathy and attentive listening. Any ties will inevitably involve misunderstandings and arguments, and how a couple handles these difficulties will frequently decide how strong and long their bond is. Emotional closeness and mutual understanding are built on open, truthful, and courteous communication.

The dynamics of love change as relationships develop, moving from the intensely passionate infatuation to a deeper, more mature kind of love. Intimacy, passion, and commitment are the three elements of love identified by psychologist Robert Sternberg's Triangular Theory of Love. Long-term relationship maintenance is called commitment, passion includes physical and emotional desire, and intimacy is the degree of emotional closeness and connection between partners. Different arrangements of these elements produce various kinds of love: companionate love (commitment and intimacy), consummate love (a balance of all three), and passionate love (passion and intimacy).

The journey of love is not without its challenges, and relationships often face periods of stress, conflicts, and external pressures. Effective conflict resolution, compromise, and resilience are vital skills that contribute to the durability of a relationship. Building a solid foundation of trust is equally crucial, as trust forms the bedrock of emotional safety and security. Trust is earned through consistent honesty, reliability, and the demonstration of mutual respect.

Love also intertwines with individual growth and self-discovery. Healthy relationships encourage personal development, fostering an environment where partners can pursue their goals, aspirations, and passions. In a relationship, self-discovery is being aware of one's requirements and those of one's partner while also coming to terms with one's needs and boundaries. A harmonious balance between individual autonomy and shared goals creates a dynamic and fulfilling relationship.

The role of love in long-term relationships extends beyond the romantic and passionate aspects. Companionship, shared values, and a sense of partnership contribute to the enduring nature of committed relationships. Building a life together involves navigating various milestones, such as marriage, parenthood, and career changes. These transitions require adaptability, mutual support, and a shared vision for the future. Couples who can navigate these life stages with resilience and unity often find their love deepens and matures over time.

While the journey of love is profoundly rewarding, it is not immune to external factors that may pose challenges. Economic pressures, societal expectations, and cultural influences can impact relationships. For instance, societal norms regarding gender roles, marriage, and family structures may shape the expectations and dynamics within a relationship. Couples may also face external stressors, such as work-related demands, financial strain, or health issues, which can pressure the relationship.

Cultural variations contribute to the diversity of love and relationship dynamics worldwide. Cultures may have unique norms, rituals, and expectations regarding courtship, marriage, and familial responsibilities. Understanding and respecting these cultural nuances is crucial for fostering cross-cultural relationships and promoting inclusivity. The diversity of love stories across cultures adds richness to the collective human experience, highlighting the universality of emotions while celebrating the unique expressions of love within different cultural contexts.

The concept of love extends beyond romantic partnerships to encompass various forms of love, including familial, spiritual, and self-love. Family love, rooted in the bonds of kinship, plays a pivotal role in shaping one's sense of identity, belonging, and support. Sibling relationships, parent-child dynamics, and extended family connections contribute to the mosaic of familial love, offering a foundation of emotional security and interconnectedness.

Platonic love, often celebrated in friendships, reflects the deep emotional bonds formed outside romance. Mutual respect, shared interests, and emotional support characterize friendships. These relationships contribute to emotional well-being, providing companionship, laughter, and a sense of belonging. Platonic love transcends societal expectations and often endures the tests of time, offering a profound connection between individuals.

One of the most important aspects of total well-being is self-love, which is developing a loving and supportive connection with oneself. It encompasses self-acceptance, self-compassion, and the practice of prioritizing one's physical, emotional, and mental health. Healthy self-love forms the basis for fulfilling relationships with others, as individuals comfortable with themselves are better equipped to create and maintain meaningful connections.

The intersection of love and psychology delves into the depths of human behavior, cognition, and emotions, offering insights into the mechanisms that govern romantic relationships. Attachment theory, pioneered by psychologists John Bowlby and Mary Ainsworth, explores the patterns of attachment individuals develop in early childhood and how these patterns influence adult relationships. Secure attachment is associated with healthy relationship dynamics, while insecure attachment may manifest as anxious or avoidant behaviors in adulthood.

Another psychological perspective on love is Sternberg's Triangular Theory, which posits that love combines intimacy, passion, and commitment. This framework offers a nuanced understanding of the multifaceted nature of love, acknowledging that relationships may shift in their emphasis on these components over time. Additionally, social cognitive theories examine the role of observational learning, socialization, and cultural influences in shaping individuals' relationship attitudes and behaviors.

The interplay of love and hormones adds a biological dimension to understanding romantic attraction and bonding. The release of chemicals such as oxytocin, serotonin, and dopamine contribute to the feelings of pleasure, happiness, and attachment associated with love. These neurochemical processes underscore the profound impact of love on the brain, influencing mood, motivation, and overall well-being.

The study of love also intersects with sociology, exploring how societal structures, norms, and expectations shape relationship dynamics. Societal influences may manifest in various ways, including cultural expectations regarding gender roles, societal attitudes toward marriage, and the impact of socioeconomic factors on relationship stability. Examining the societal context provides a holistic view of the factors contributing to the diverse expressions of love within different communities and cultures.

Love in literature and the arts is a timeless muse, inspiring countless poems, novels, paintings, and musical compositions. From Shakespearean sonnets to classic love stories, artistic expressions capture the myriad facets of love—its joys, sorrows, complexities, and transcendent qualities. The arts mirror the human experience, reflecting the depth and breadth of emotions accompanying the love journey.

In conclusion, love and relationships constitute a multifaceted and transformative aspect of the human experience. From the initial sparks of attraction to the enduring bonds forged through commitment, the journey of love encompasses a rich tapestry of emotions, challenges, and personal growth. Understanding love's psychological, emotional, and sociocultural dynamics provides insightful observations about the nuances of human connection. Whether exploring the intricacies of romantic relationships, the enduring bonds of family, the joys of friendship, or the importance of self-love, exploring love unveils its profound impact on individuals and the collective fabric of human society. Through the lenses of psychology, biology, sociology, and the arts, the study of love invites us to unravel the mysteries of the heart, celebrating the diverse expressions of this universal and enduring human experience.

Prosperity and Abundance

Prosperity and abundance, while often associated with material wealth, extend far beyond the realm of finances, encompassing a holistic and multifaceted approach to life. The pursuit of prosperity involves the cultivation of a mindset, the alignment of one's energies, and the recognition of abundance in various aspects of existence. It is a philosophy that transcends mere financial gain, emphasizing the enrichment of one's overall well-being, relationships, and spiritual fulfillment.

At its core, prosperity consciousness is rooted in the belief that abundance is not a finite resource but an infinite and accessible state of being. This mindset asserts that there is more than enough to go around, encouraging individuals to change their perspective from lack to abundance. Embracing this perspective involves acknowledging the interconnectedness of all aspects of life and recognizing the potential for growth, success, and fulfillment in various domains.

The journey toward prosperity often begins with self-awareness and a conscious examination of one's beliefs and thought patterns. Negative and limiting beliefs, often ingrained in societal conditioning or past experiences, can create barriers to prosperity. These beliefs may manifest as doubts about one's worthiness, fears of scarcity, or self-imposed limitations on success. Identifying and challenging these limiting beliefs is crucial in fostering a mindset that welcomes prosperity.

Positive affirmations, visualization, and mindfulness practices are potent tools for cultivating a prosperous mindset. Affirmations, repeated statements that reinforce positive beliefs, serve to reprogram the subconscious mind, replacing limiting thoughts with empowering ones. Visualization involves creating vivid mental images of desired outcomes, allowing the mind to align with the energy of abundance. Mindfulness practices, such as meditation, promote present-moment awareness, reducing stress and opening the mind to the possibilities in the here and now.

In the realm of prosperity and abundance, the law of attraction plays a pivotal role. This universal principle posits that like attracts like, suggesting that the energy one puts into the world influences the experiences and opportunities that come back. By maintaining a positive and abundant mindset, individuals may attract circumstances, people, and resources that align with their vibrational frequency. The law of attraction underscores the importance of conscious intention-setting and recognizing the power of thoughts and emotions in shaping one's reality.

Material wealth is undoubtedly a component of prosperity, and financial abundance is often a tangible expression of success and well-being. However, pursuing prosperity extends beyond monetary gain to encompass a broader abundance spectrum. Health and well-being, meaningful relationships, personal growth, and a sense of purpose are integral to a prosperous life. Recognizing and appreciating these diverse forms of abundance contributes to a more holistic and fulfilling experience.

The concept of prosperity is deeply intertwined with abundance in relationships. Healthy and harmonious connections with others contribute significantly to an enriched life. Meaningful relationships provide emotional support, companionship, and a sense of belonging. Cultivating strong social bonds involves qualities such as empathy, effective communication, and a willingness to contribute positively to the well-being of others. The abundance of love, kindness, and shared experiences in relationships amplifies the overall sense of prosperity.

Furthermore, personal growth and continuous learning are essential elements of a prosperous life. Pursuing knowledge, skills, and self-improvement contributes to a sense of fulfillment and accomplishment. Embracing challenges, learning from experiences, and expanding one's horizons foster a mindset of growth and resilience. The abundance of learning and personal development opportunities adds depth and richness to the journey toward prosperity.

Spiritual fulfillment is another dimension of prosperity that goes beyond the material realm. This component is feeling a sense of belonging to something bigger than oneself, such as the universe, a higher power, or a more precise grasp of one's purpose. Spiritual exercises like thought, prayer, and meditation offer ways to delve into this aspect of plenty. The richness of inner calm, thankfulness, and a spiritual connection influences overall prosperity.

In the pursuit of prosperity, the importance of gratitude cannot be overstated. Gratitude is a transformative force that shifts focus from what is lacking to what is present. Cultivating a habit of expressing gratitude for the abundance already present in one's life enhances awareness of the positive aspects of existence. Gratitude acts as a magnet, drawing more of what is appreciated into one's experience. This simple yet profound practice fosters a mindset of abundance, attracting additional blessings and opportunities.

In work and career, prosperity consciousness influences professional success and fulfillment. Thinking of issues as opportunities rather than barriers encourages creativity, adaptability, and taking the initiative to overcome them. People with a prosperous mindset see their jobs as professional and personal development opportunities rather than just a way to get money. This strategy, which emphasizes purpose and contribution, frequently results in a more satisfying and gratifying job.

Entrepreneurship, emphasizing innovation and value creation, aligns closely with the principles of prosperity. Entrepreneurs who approach their ventures with a mindset of abundance are more likely to navigate challenges creatively and attract growth opportunities. The ability to see beyond immediate setbacks, adapt to changing circumstances, and maintain a positive vision for the future contributes to the sustained success of entrepreneurial endeavors.

In the realm of prosperity, philanthropy and giving back play a significant role. Being aware that wealth is meant to be shared encourages civic engagement and a sense of social responsibility. Acts of generosity, whether through charitable contributions, volunteerism, or mentorship, create a positive ripple effect. The abundance of resources, skills, and knowledge shared with others contributes to the collective well-being of communities and society.

The principles of prosperity extend beyond individual pursuits to impact societal structures and economic systems. A paradigm shift from a scarcity-based economic model to one that embraces sustainability, inclusivity, and equitable distribution of resources aligns with the philosophy of prosperity for all. Such a shift involves reevaluating societal values, prioritizing environmental stewardship, and creating economic systems prioritizing the well-being of individuals and the planet.

In conclusion, prosperity and abundance encompass a multifaceted and transformative approach to life beyond material wealth accumulation. A prosperity mindset involves cultivating positive beliefs, embracing the law of attraction, and recognizing abundance in various aspects of existence. Beyond financial gain, prosperity extends to holistic well-being, meaningful relationships, personal growth, and spiritual fulfillment. The principles of prosperity influence professional success, entrepreneurial endeavors, and societal structures, emphasizing the interconnectedness of individual and collective well-being. Through gratitude, philanthropy, and a commitment to shared prosperity, individuals contribute to a more enriching and fulfilling experience for themselves and the world around them. When approached with mindfulness and intention, Prosperity becomes a guiding philosophy that empowers individuals to lead purposeful, abundant lives.

Protection and Cleansing

Protection and cleansing rituals have been integral components of various cultural and spiritual traditions throughout history, serving as practices aimed at safeguarding individuals, spaces, and energies from negative influences. Rooted in the belief that spiritual and energetic well-being is intertwined with overall health and prosperity, these rituals often involve symbolic actions, sacred tools, and the invocation of higher powers. Whether fending off evil forces, dispelling negative energies, or creating holy spaces, protection and cleansing rituals offer diverse practices that address well-being's spiritual, psychological, and emotional dimensions.

One common thread across different cultures is the recognition of the existence of negative energies or entities that can impact individuals and their environments. In many belief systems, it is believed that these energies can manifest as spiritual disturbances, psychic attacks, or even evil entities. Protection rituals, therefore, are designed to create a shield of spiritual defense, offering a layer of safeguarding against external or internal sources of negativity.

The use of sacred tools is a prevalent feature in protection rituals. These tools vary across traditions, including crystals, herbs, amulets, talismans, or ceremonial objects charged with specific energies. For instance, certain crystals are believed to possess protective properties in crystal healing. Black tourmaline is often utilized for its ability to absorb and transmute negative energies, while clear quartz is valued for its amplifying properties that enhance protective intentions. Similarly, herbs such as sage, cedar, or frankincense are burned as cleansing agents in various cultural practices to purify spaces and dispel negative energies.

Cleansing is deeply ingrained in many spiritual traditions through rituals, ceremonies, or specific practices. Cleansing rituals remove stagnant or harmful energies, purify spaces, and restore balance and harmony. These rituals often involve elements like water, fire, earth, and air, each representing different aspects of purification.

In many indigenous cultures, smudging ceremonies are standard purification practices. It is said that burning bundles of dried herbs, such as sweetgrass or sage, and spreading the smoke over a room will purge negative energy and produce a spiritually pure atmosphere. This custom stems from the idea that smoke conveys messages to the divine and helps open doors between the spiritual and material worlds. Revered for its purifying properties, water is frequently incorporated into cleansing rituals. Ritual baths, water blessings, or even washing one's hands can symbolize cleansing. The concept of holy water in various religious traditions, used for blessings and purifications, is an example of water's significance in spiritual cleansing practices.

With its transformative and purifying qualities, fire is another elemental force commonly utilized in cleansing rituals. Candle magic, for instance, involves using candles to focus intentions and dispel negative energies. The flame is seen as a symbol of transformation, consuming negativity and illuminating the path towards positivity and clarity.

Earth, symbolizing stability and grounding, is often integrated into cleansing practices. Salt, considered a purifying agent, is sprinkled in spaces or used in protective circles to create a barrier against harmful influences. Burial or grounding rituals involving burying specific items are also employed to neutralize unwanted energies and restore balance.

Air, associated with breath and life force, is harnessed in cleansing rituals through practices such as smudging, where the wafting of smoke is considered to carry away negative energies. The power of breath is harnessed in mindfulness and meditation practices, where conscious breathing is used to release stress and purify the mind.

In addition to elemental rituals, many protection and cleansing practices involve invoking spiritual entities or deities. Prayers, invocations, or mantras are recited in various religious traditions to seek divine protection and guidance. For example, casting a protective circle and invoking deities or elemental forces in Wiccan rituals are standard practices to create a sacred and protected space.

Amulets and talismans, believed to carry protective energies, are often employed as wearable or carryable items. These may include symbols, charms, or crafted objects charged with specific mentions for protection. Wearing a religious pendant, a sacred symbol, or a gemstone believed to possess protective properties is practiced in diverse cultures worldwide.

The belief in the harmful effects of envious or malevolent looks is reflected in the idea of the evil eye, which is common in many cultures. The Nazar in Turkish culture and the Hamsa hand in Middle Eastern traditions are examples of talismans meant to ward off the evil eye. These are protective symbols used to divert harmful energies and keep people safe.

While protection and cleansing rituals are deeply embedded in spiritual and religious practices, their relevance extends beyond these contexts. In modern times, individuals from various spiritual backgrounds and those who may not identify with a particular faith incorporate these rituals into their lives as tools for self-care and mental well-being. The emphasis on mindfulness, intention-setting, and creating positive environments aligns with contemporary approaches to holistic health.

Energy healing techniques like Reiki and crystal healing incorporate cleansing and protection techniques as core elements of their approaches. Before a session, Reiki practitioners frequently clear their workspaces and energy fields. Crystals used in energy therapy are often cleansed and charged to preserve their energetic purity and potency.

Psychological perspectives on protection and cleansing rituals emphasize the impact of intention and symbolism on the human psyche. The placebo effect, where individuals experience positive outcomes due to their beliefs and expectations, is relevant in the context of these rituals. The psychological benefits of feeling protected, grounded, and spiritually cleansed contribute to an individual's well-being and resilience.

It is also acknowledged that mindfulness exercises like visualization and meditation have purifying and safeguarding effects. These techniques support people in developing stress relief, mental clarity, and present-moment awareness. People can strengthen their mental and emotional health by imagining a shield of protection and concentrating on good intentions.

In conclusion, protection and cleansing rituals represent a rich tapestry of practices deeply ingrained in various cultural, spiritual, and holistic traditions. Whether through invoking higher powers, sacred tools, elemental rituals, or psychological approaches, these practices safeguard individuals and spaces from negative influences. Beyond their spiritual or religious contexts, these rituals resonate with modern well-being practices, energy healing modalities, and psychological well-being approaches. The universality of the human experience is reflected in the shared understanding that maintaining spiritual and energetic hygiene is integral to a balanced and harmonious life. As individuals navigate the complexities of the modern world, the enduring appeal of protection and cleansing rituals attests to their timeless significance in fostering holistic well-being.

CHAPTER VI

Rituals for Each Moon Phase

New Moon Ritual for Setting Intentions

The New Moon, a celestial phenomenon when the moon is not visible from Earth, symbolizes a potent moment for fresh beginnings and the seeding of intentions. In many spiritual and cultural traditions, the New Moon is a decisive moment for wishing, setting goals, and beginning new cycles. A lunar cycle begins during this moon phase, providing a blank slate with favorable energy for sowing the seeds of aspirations, objectives, and manifestations. Setting intentions during a New Moon ritual is a technique that aligns with the moon's cyclical cycle and the ebb and flow of cosmic energies.

At the heart of the New Moon ritual is intention setting— a mindful and deliberate act of clarifying what one wishes to manifest or cultivate in one's life. Intention setting involves identifying specific goals, aspirations, or qualities that align with one's values and desired path. During the New Moon, the energy particularly supports this process, offering a unique opportunity to tap into the Fert Le's potential for new beginnings.

The ritual often begins by creating a sacred space. This can be a quiet corner of a room, an outdoor setting, or any place where one feels a sense of tranquility and connection. The cleansing is symbolic, representing the clearing away of the old to make room for the new.

As the sacred space is established, individuals may engage in centering practices such as meditation or deep breathing. These practices help to calm the mind, enhance focus, and create a receptive state for the intention-setting process. The New Moon, often associated with a sense of introspection and calm, provides an ideal backdrop for turning inward and aligning with one's inner wisdom.

The use of symbolic tools and elements is a prevalent aspect of New Moon rituals. Crystals, with their energetic properties, are often employed to amplify intentions. For example, clear quartz may enhance clarity and focus, while rose quartz could be chosen for intentions related to love and relationship hips. Placing these crystals in the ritual space or holding them during the intention-setting process serves to imbue the energy of the stones into the intentions.

Candles are another standard tool in New Moon rituals. The flickering flame symbolizes transformation and the illumination of one's path. Lighting a candle during the ritual enhances the ambiance and represents igniting one's intentions. The act of candle magic, where specific colors correspond to different intentions, adds a layer of symbolism and focus to the ritual.

Incorporating elements of nature is a meaningful aspect of New Moon rituals. Although not visible, the moon is acknowledged as a potent celestial presence. Moon-gazing or spending time outdoors under the night sky during the New Moon can deepen the connection to lunar energies. Some individuals collect water, either dew or rain, during the New Moon, considering it is charged with the moon's energy and suitable for cleansing or blessing. Journaling is a critical component of many New Moon rituals. Writing down intentions, dreams, and aspirations is a powerful way to externalize inner desires and anchor them in the material realm. Putting pen to paper engages the analytical and creative aspects of the mind, clarifying intentions and solidifying the commitment to manifest them. Some individuals also create a New Moon vision board, collaging images and words representing their intentions.

The practice of affirmations is often integrated into New Moon rituals. Affirmations are positive statements framed in the present tense that align with one's intentions. By repeating these affirmations during the ritual, individuals reinforce the vibrational frequency of their desires, fostering a greater sense of belief and alignment with the intended manifestations.

The timing of a New Moon ritual is considered significant. While the New Moon is optimal for intention setting, the energy is typically felt strongest within the first 48 hours after the New Moon. This period is often called the "waxing crescent" phase, where the moon begins to reveal a tiny sliver of its illuminated side. The wax ng crescent signifies the initial growth and building of intentions, making it a suitable time for action and forward momentum.

For example, a New Moon in Aries may be associated with courage, initiative, and new beginnings, while a New Moon in Pisces may emphasize intuition, creativity, and spiritual pursuits. Astrology enthusiasts may align their intentions with the qualities associated with the specific zodiac sign of the New Moon.

The actual process of setting intentions during a New Moon ritual involves a thoughtful and intentional approach. Individuals may reflect on different areas of their lives, such as relationships, careers, health, or personal growth, and craft intentions that resonate with their aspirations in each area. It is essential to phrase intentions positively, affirming what is desired rather than lacking or to be avoided.

During the ritual, as intentions are articulated, individuals infuse them with emotion and a genuine sense of belief. The emotional charge adds a dynamic energy to the intentions, aligning them with the heart's desires. Visualization, a powerful tool in manifestation practices, involves mentally picturing the desired outcomes as if they are already occurring and engaging the senses and emotions. At the same time, visualizing deepens the impact of the intention-setting process.

In some New Moon rituals, individuals may perform a ritualized act to symbolize anchoring their intentions. This act could be lighting a candle, burying symbolic objects, or even creating a small altar dedicated to the intentions. The ritualized act physically represents the commitment to manifesting the intentions into reality.

Consistency is a crucial aspect of successful intention setting during New Moon rituals. While the New Moon provides a potent window for initiation, the ongoing commitment to the intentions through daily practices, affirmations, and inspired actions sustains the momentum. Revisiting and reflecting on the intentions regularly reinforces the connection to the desired outcomes.

As the lunar cycle progresses, the subsequent phases offer reflection, adjustment, and celebration opportunities. Following the New Moon, the waxing crescent phase is a time for taking inspired actions and nurturing the growth of intentions. The first quarter moon invites a reassessment of intentions and any necessary adjustments, while the full moon marks a culmination and fruition of intentions. The waning phases provide a period for release, letting go of what no longer serves, and preparing for the upcoming New Moon.

In conclusion, the New Moon ritual for setting intentions is a profound and timeless practice that aligns individuals with the cyclical energies of the moon and the potential for new beginnings. Rooted in mindfulness, symbolism, and the understanding of cosmic influences, this ritual provides a sacred space for the conscious creation of one's reality. Whether through the use of crystals, candles, journaling, or affirmations, each element contributes to the rich tapestry of the ritual, infusing it with personal meaning and intention. As individuals engage in this intentional practice, they embrace the opportunity to co-create their lives with the cosmic forces that govern the universe, tapping into the limitless potential that the New Moon offers for manifestation and growth.

Full Moon Esbat Rritual for Manifestation

In many spiritual and mystical traditions, the Full Moon—a celestial spectacle that occurs when the moon is completely illuminated in the night sky—has particular importance. This lunar phase, often associated with heightened energy and illumination, provides a powerful backdrop for rituals and ceremonies. Among these rituals, the Full Moon Esbat ritual for manifestation stands out as a practice that harnesses the potent energies of the moon to amplify intentions and bring desired outcomes to fruition. Rooted in the belief that the Full Moon is a time of culmination, abundance, and heightened spiritual energy, this ritual aligns practitioners with the cyclical nature of the moon and the expansive potential for manifestation.

"Esbat" is derived from Old French and refers to a meeting or gathering. In modern Pagan and Wiccan traditions, an Esbat is a ritual gathering, often held during the Full Moon, dedicated to magical workings, celebrations, and communing with the divine. The Full Moon Esbat ritual for manifestation is a focused and intentional ceremony within this broader tradition, emphasizing the power of the Full Moon to amplify intentions and catalyze the manifestation process.

Creating a sacred space is foundational to the Full Moon Esbat ritual. T involves choosing a quiet and undisturbed location, indoors or outdoors, where practitioners can connect with the energy of the F ll Moon. Cleansing the space using methods like smudging with sage, palo santo, or other purifying herbs is common. The cleansing symbolizes removing stagnant energies and preparing a spiritually changed environment.

Like many rituals, the Full Moon Esbat often begins with a grounding and centering practice. This can involve deep breathing, meditation, or visualization exercises to bring participants into a state of presence and receptivity. The heightened energy of the Full Moon creates a conducive atmosphere for heightened awareness and connection with the divine forces.

Symbolic tools and elements are integral to the Full Moon Esbat ritual. Crystals, known for their energetic properties, are frequently incorporated to enhance the energies of the ritual. Practitioners may choose crystals that align with their specific intentions for manifestation. For instance, amethyst may be used for spiritual growth, citrine for abundance, or rose quartz for heart matters. Placing these crystals in the ritual space or holding them during the ceremony helps infuse the stones' energies into the manifestation process.

Candles, associated with illumination and transformation, are another standard tool in Full Moo rituals. Lighting candles symbolizes bringing light to one's intentions and the manifestation process. Candle colors can further align with specific intentions; for example, green for abundance, red for passion, or white for clarity. The flickering flame becomes a focal point, representing the ignition and amplification of intentions.

With its profound influence on Earth's energies, the moon takes center stage in the Full Moon Esbat ritual. Moon-gazing or spending time outdoors under the luminous night sky fosters a direct connection with lunar energies. Some practitioners charge objects like crystals or water by placing them under the Full moon's glow, believing they absorb the potent lunar energies for later use in the ritual or for personal energy work.

Water, often associated with the moon and its cyclical rhythms, is symbolic in Full Moon rituals. Moonwater, created by leaving water in a container under the Full Moon, is believed to carry the moon's energy and can be used for cleansing and charging ritual tools. Including a bowl of moon water in the ritual space adds a layer of lunar symbolism and energetic resonance.

The ritual act of casting a circle is a common practice in man Esbat rituals. The circle represents a sacred and protected space, a barrier that separates the mundane from the magical. The casing of the circle can be accompanied by invocations to the four directions, elements, or deities, depending on the practitioner's spiritual tradition. The circular boundary serves as a container for the ritual energies, creating a focused and consecrated space for manifestation.

A vital element of the Full Moon Esbat ritual is articulating intentions. Participants take turns expressing their desires, goals, and aspirations, speaking them aloud to the moon and the divine forces present. The Full Moon, associated with the culmination of energy and the peak of its influence, amplifies these intentions. Speaking with attention adds another layer of manifestation energy since spoken words are said to have a specific vibrational frequency that affects the energetic domain.

Like those you saw in New Moon rituals, affirmations are often integrated into Full Moon Esbat ceremonies. These positive statements, framed in the present tense and aligned with one's intentions, contribute to the manifestation process. Repetitioning affirmations during the ritual reinforces the desired outcomes, fostering a greater sense of belief and alignment with the intentions.

Visualization, a powerful tool in manifestation practices, is particularly potent during the Full Moon. Participants are encouraged to mentally picture the fulfillment of their intentions as vividly as possible. Engaging the senses and emotions while visualizing deepens the impact of the manifestation process, creating a robust and energetic connection between the practitioner and the desired outcomes.

Practitioners may perform symbolic acts in some Full Moon Esbat rituals to anchor their intentions. This could involve physically presenting the desired outcome, such as a vision board or an extended object charged with intention. The ritualized act becomes a tangible expression of commitment and belief in the manifestation process.

Astrological considerations may influence the timing and themes of Full Moon sbat rituals. The zodiac sign in which the Full Moon occurs adds energy and influence to the intentions. For example, a Full Moon in Taurus may emphasize grounding, stability, and material manifestations, while a Full Moon in Scorpio may highlight transformation, depth, and emotional healing. Astrology enthusiasts may align their intentions with the qualities associated with the scientific zodiac sign of the Full Moon.

Energy-raising activities often accompany the Full Moon Esbat ritual. Chanting, drumming, or dancing can elevate the energetic vibrations in the ritual space, intensifying the connection with the Full Moon's potent energies. The rhythmic and intentional movement aligns participants with the flow of cosmic energies, enhancing the manifestation process.

The culmination time of the Full Moon Esbat ritual often involves a closing ceremony. This may include expressions of gratitude to the moon, the divine forces invoked, and the participants in the ritual. The closing of the ritual circle is a deliberate act, signifying the end of the focused magical work and the return to the mundane world. So, practitioners release excess energy raised during the ritual, grounding themselves by changing the earth or the ground.

Consistent reflection on intentions and actions is encouraged in the days and weeks following the Full Moon Esbat ritual. The Full Moon's energy extends beyond the night of the ritual, offering a window of opportunity for manifestation in the subsequent lunar phases. Practitioners may find it beneficial to revisit their intentions regularly, assess pro ress, and make necessary adjustments or refinements.

In conclusion, the Full Moon Esbat ritual for manifestation is a dynamic and intentional practice that aligns participants with the potent energies of the Full Moon. Rooted in symbolism, lunar associations, and the belief in the amplifying power of the Full Moon, this ritual provides a sacred space for Conscio's manifestation. Whether through the use of crystals, candles, affirmations, or symbolic acts, each element contributes to the rich tapestry of the ritual, infusing it with personal meaning and intention. As participants engage in this intentional practice, they tap into the expansive and abundant energies of the Full Moon, co-creating their reality and bringing their most profound desires to fruition.

Waning Moon Ritual for Letting Go

When the moon's illumination diminishes from complete to new, the waning moon marks a period associated with release, reflection, and letting go. In various spiritual and mystical traditions, the waning moon is a time to shed what no longer serves, clear stagnant energies, and make space for new beginnings. The Waning Moon Ritual for Letting Go is a practice rooted in the understanding that the lunar cycle mirrors the cyclical nature of life, encouraging individuals to align their personal growth and transformation with the moon's rhythms.

Creating a sacred space is foundational to the Waning Moon Ritual for Letting Go. The chosen indoor or outdoor space serves as a container for the release and purification. Clearing the space with methods like smudging or burning purifying herbs symbolizes removing lingering energies and preparing the environment for intentional letting go. Cleansing signifies a fresh start and a commitment to release what is no longer needed.

Grounding and centering practices are often incorporated into the Waning Moon Ritual to bring participants into a state of presence and receptivity. These practices may include deep breathing exercises, meditation, or visualization to anchor individuals in the present moment. The waning moon's energy supports introspection, making it a suitable time for reflection on aspects of life that need release or transformation.

Symbolic tools and elements play a significant role in the Waning Moon Ritual. Crystals, known for their energetic properties, are often utilized to enhance the energies of the ritual. Black obsidian, for example, is considered a powerful stone for letting go and releasing negativity, while moonstone is linked to emotional equilibrium and intuition. Placing these crystals in the ritual space or holding them during the ceremony helps to amplify the energies of the letting process.

Candles, with their transformative qualities, are commonly used in Waning Moon rituals. Lighting candles symbolize the darkness's illumination and the release process's initiation. The flame represents the burning away of old patterns or energies, making space for renewal. Some practitioners choose candles of specific colors that correspond to their intentions, such as black for banishing negativity or white for purification.

The ritual casting of a circle is a common practice in Waning Moon ceremonies. The circle is a sacred and protected space, creating a boundary between the mundane and the magical. Casting the circle is often accompanied by invocations to the four directions, elements, or deities, depending on the practitioner's spiritual tradition. The circular boundary signifies containment for the release work and establishes a consecrated space.

Water, symbolizing purification and emotional release, is significant in Waning Moon rituals. Ritual baths or the use of consecrated water can enhance the cleansing process. Immersing oneself in water during the ritual or incorporating water in other forms, such as placing a bowl of consecrated water in the ritual space, adds a watery and emotional dimension to the letting process.

Releasing and letting go is crucial to the Waning Moon Ritual. It is advised for participants to consider areas of their lives that they would like to let go of, such as bad thought patterns, unhealthful relationships, or ingrained routines. Articulating these aspects aloud during the ritual serves as an acknowledgment and a commitment to the release process. The spoken word carries a unique vibrational frequency that aligns to let go.

Affirmations tailored for letting go are often integrated into the Waning Moon Ritual. These positive statements, framed in the present tense, support the release process by affirming the desire to release and create space for positive change. The repetition of these affirmations during the ritual reinforces the intention and shifts the energetic vibrations toward the desired outcome.

Visualization, a powerful tool in manifestation and release practices, is particularly potent during the waning moon. Participants are guided to visualize the release process as a symbolic or metaphorical act. This could involve visualizing old patterns dissolving, negativity being carried away by a flowing river, or envisioning a dark cloud life revealing clear skies. Engaging the senses and emotions during visualization deepens the impact of the release process.

The ritualized act of physically letting go is often incorporated into the Waning Moon ceremony. Participants may choose symbolic objects to represent what they want to release, such as written notes, images, or objects charged with specific energies. These objects may be burned, buried, or released into flowing water as a tangible and intentional expression of letting go.

Astrological considerations may influence the timing and themes of Waning Moon rituals. The zodiac sign in which the moon is waning adds a layer of energy and influence to the release intentions. For example, a waning moon in Scorpio may emphasize letting go of emotional baggage and transforming deep-seated patterns. In contrast, a waning moon in Capricorn may highlight the release of old structures and limitations. Astrology enthusiasts may align their real intentions with the qualities associated with the specific zodiac sign of the waning moon.

The culmination of the Waning Moon Ritual often involves a closing ceremony. This may include gratitude for the release process, acknowledgment of the space held during the ritual, and a sense of closure. The closing of the ritual circle is a deliberate act, signaling the end of the focused magical work and the return to the mundane world. Participants may choose to ground themselves by connecting with the earth or performing a ritualized act to symbolize completing the release process.

Consistent reflection on the release intentions and the resulting changes is encouraged in the days and weeks following the Waning Moon Ri ul. The waning moon's energy extends beyond the night of the ritual, providing an ongoing opportunity for release and transformation in the subsequent lunar phases. Practitioners may find it beneficial to revisit their release in entions regularly, assess progress, and make necessary adjustments or refinements.

In conclusion, the Waning Moon Ritual for Letting Go is a poignant and intentional practice that aligns individuals with the cyclical energies of the waning moon. Rooted in symbolism, lunar associations, and the belief in the transformative power of release, this ritual provides a sacred space for conscious letting go. Whether through the use of crystals, candles, affirmations, or symbolic acts, each element contributes to the rich tapestry of the ritual, infusing it with personal meaning and intention. As participants engage in this intentional practice, they tap into the releasing and transformative energies of the waning moon, allowing them to shed what no longer serves and make space for new beginnings and growth.

CHAPTER VII

Moonlit Divination

Lunar Tarot Spreads

Lunar Tarot spreads offer a unique and insightful approach to divination, intertwining the Tarot's wisdom with the Moon's cyclical energies. Rooted in the belief that both the Tarot and lunar phases provide valuable guidance and reflection, these spreads offer practitioners a nuanced way to explore their inner landscapes, navigate life's cycles, and align with the mystical influences of the Moon. Combining these two robust systems creates a rich tapestry of symbolism and meaning, inviting individuals to connect with the ebb and flow of their spiritual journey.

One expected Lunar Tarot spread is the New Moon Spread, specifically designed to harness the energy of new beginnings and intentions associated with the New Moon phase. This spread typically consists of positions representing the energies of the New Moon, the waxing crescent, and the first quarter moon. Cards drawn in each position offer insights into the individual's current state, potential obstacles, and the energies supporting the initiation of new projects or endeavors. The New Moon Spread is a dynamic tool for setting intentions and gaining clarity during the early phases of a lunar cycle.

The Full Moon Spread, on the other hand, is tailored to the culmination and illumination energies of the Full Moon. This spread often features positions representing the past, present, and future aspects of the querent's life, offering a comprehensive view of their journey. The cards drawn in this spread may provide insights into what has come to fruition, what is currently illuminated, and what may be approaching completion or transformation. The

Full Moon Spread serves as a reflective tool, allowing individuals to assess their progress and gain clarity on the energies surrounding them during the peak of the lunar cycle.

Waning Moon Spreads are made to resonate with the energies of release, reflection, and letting go that are associated with the moon's waning phases. These spreads often feature positions corresponding to the aspects of life or patterns individuals wish to release, the challenges they may face in letting go, and the energies supporting their surrender. Cards drawn in each position offer guidance on the release process and insights into the transformative energies during the waning Moon. Waning Moon Spreads provides a valuable tool for navigating transitions, shedding old patterns, and making space for renewal.

Waxing Moon Spreads, conversely, focus on the energies of growth, manifestation, and expansion associated with the waxing phases of the Moon. These spreads may include positions representing the areas of life where growth is desired, potential obstacles or challenges on the path, and the supportive energies propelling the querent forward. Cards drawn in each position guide how to harness the waxing Moon's energies for personal and spiritual development. Waxing Moon Spreads are empowering tools for setting goals, cultivating abundance, and aligning with the expansive energies of the waxing phases.

The Lunar Eclipse Spread is a specialized Tarot spread designed to align with the powerful energies of a lunar eclipse. Lunar eclipses are potent moments of cosmic alignment, symbolizing moments of profound change and transformation. This spread may feature positions representing the energies of the eclipse, the aspects of life affected by the eclipse, and the potential outcomes or revelations. Cards drawn in each position offer insights into the transformative energies and guidance on navigating the shifts brought about by the lunar eclipse. The Lunar Eclipse Spread is a tool for harnessing the profound energies of these celestial events and understanding their impact on one's life journey.

Incorporating Tarot into lunar practices provides a multi-layered approach to divination, allowing individuals to weave together the archetypal symbols of the Tarot with the cyclical and mystical energies of the Moon. These Lunar Tarot spreads offer practitioners a dynamic and intuitive means of exploring their inner landscapes, gaining insights into the energies surrounding them, and aligning with the natural rhythms of life.

As individuals engage with Lunar Tarot spreads, they are invited to embrace the fluidity of life's cycles, recognizing that each phase offers unique opportunities for growth, reflection, release, and manifestation. The New Moon spreads encourage intention-setting and the initiation of new projects, aligning with the energies of beginnings and potential. A full Moon provides a moment of illumination and culmination, offering a panoramic view of one's journey and the fruits of one's efforts. Waning Moon spreads guide individuals through release, letting go, and surrendering to the transformative energies at play. Waxing Moon empowers practitioners to set goals, cultivate abundance, and align with the expansive energies of growth and manifestation.

The Lunar Eclipse Spread, focusing on celestial alignments, is a potent tool for navigating moments of profound change and transformation. Whether drawn to the energy of new beginnings, the illumination of fullness, the surrender of release, the growth of manifestation, or the transformative power of eclipses, individuals can tailor their Tarot practice to align with the specific energies of the Moon.

Lunar Tarot spreads provide practical insights and guidance and foster a deepened connection to the natural rhythms of the cosmos. The archetypal symbols of the Tarot, rich with universal meanings, seamlessly integrate with the cyclical energies of the Moon, creating a synergistic and intuitive divination practice. Through these spreads, individuals embark on self-discovery, introspection, and alignment with the mystical forces that shape their lives. As the Tarot cards are laid out in response to the phases of the Moon, a dialogue unfolds between the individual and the cosmic energies, revealing the ever- changing dance of life's cycles and the wisdom inherent in each lunar phase.

Scrying by Moonlight

Scrying by Moonlight, an ancient and mystical practice, involves gazing into reflective surfaces during the Moon's luminous phases to gain insights, receive visions, and connect with the spiritual realm. The term "scrying" is derived from the Old English word "descry," meaning to make out dimly or to reveal. Across various cultures and historical periods, scrying has been employed as a divination method, allowing individuals to access intuitive guidance, receive messages from the beyond, and tap into the subconscious mind. When coupled with the serene and enchanting energy of Moonlight, scrying takes on a heightened dimension, creating a potent synergy between the reflective properties of the chosen medium and the mystical influence of the Moon.

The choice of scrying medium is diverse, ranging from traditional tools like crystal balls and mirrors to natural elements like water and even flames. With its ethereal glow, Moonlight adds enchantment to the scrying experience, enhancing the practitioner's receptivity to subtle energies and intuitive insights. Scrying by Moonlight is deeply intertwined with the esoteric and spiritual traditions that recognize the Moon's influence on psychic abilities, intuition, and the mysteries of the subconscious.

One of the most iconic scrying tools is the crystal ball, a sphere of clear quartz or other translucent stones. The crystal ball is a focal point for the scrying practitioner, who gazes into its depths to access visions and impressions. When performed under the Moonlight, the crystal ball reflects the lunar energies, infusing the scrying session with a heightened sense of mystery and intuition. The Moon's cycles, from the waxing crescent to the full Moon and the waning phases, are believed to influence the potency and nature of the visions received during scrying. With their reflective surfaces, mirrors have also been used for scrying throughout history. The Moon's soft glow lends a subtle illumination to the mirror, creating an atmospheric and conducive environment for scrying. Practitioners often dim the surrounding light and position the mirror to capture the Moon's radiance, allowing its energy to enhance the scrying experience. As a portal to the subconscious and spiritual realms, the mirror becomes a dynamic tool for receiving insights and divinatory messages under the moonlit sky.

Water scrying, known as hydromancy, involves gazing into a bowl of water, a natural body of water, or a scrying mirror placed above a bowl of water. The Moon's reflection on the water's surface adds an enchanting quality to the practice, as if the practitioner is peering into the liminal space between the physical and spiritual realms. Moonlight dances on the water, creating ripples of illumination that enhance the practitioner's receptivity to symbolic imagery and intuitive messages. Hydromancy by Moonlight taps into the ancient associations between water, the Moon, and the fluidity of the psychic realms.

Flame scrying, or pyromancy, utilizes the flickering flames of candles or fire as a scrying medium. The dance of the flames in the moonlit darkness creates a dynamic and mesmerizing setting for scrying. Practitioners focus on the shifting shapes and shadows within the fire, allowing their minds to open to symbolic visions and messages. The Moon, as a silent witness to the sacred dance of fire, adds an otherworldly quality to the pyromantic scrying experience, deepening the connection between the practitioner and the spiritual energies invoked.

The phases of the moon greatly influence moonlight scrying, with each phase said to improve particular facets of the technique. During the waxing phases, from the new Moon to the full Moon, practitioners often find that the Moon's increasing luminosity intensifies their intuitive receptivity. It is a time conducive to initiating new insights, setting intentions, and receiving guidance on matters of growth and manifestation. The full Moon, in particular, is regarded as a peak moment for scrying, as its radiant glow symbolizes the culmination of energies and the revelation of hidden truths.

Conversely, the waning phases of the Moon, from the full Moon to the new Moon, are associated with the energies of release, reflection, and letting go. Scrying during this period may be focused on gaining insights into what needs to be released or surrendered. The decreasing Moonlight during the waning phases is an opportunity to delve into the subconscious, uncover hidden patterns, and receive guidance on the art of surrender and transformation.

The practice of scrying by Moonlight is deeply intertwined with the belief in the Moon's influence on psychic abilities. The Moon, long associated with the feminine and intuitive aspects of existence, is believed to amplify the channels between the conscious and subconscious mind during scrying sessions. As the Moonlight bathes the scrying medium, it is thought to activate the intuitive centers within the practitioner, allowing them to access deeper layers of insight and revelation.

Moonlight scrying is not solely about predicting the future or obtaining specific answers; it is also a process of self-discovery and spiritual communion. The Moon, as a symbol of cycles, reflection, and illumination, mirrors the soul's journey. Scrying by Moonlight becomes a sacred dance between the individual and the cosmic energies, an exploration of the unseen realms, and a communion with the mysteries that dwell in the shadows and reflections.

In preparing for a scrying by moonlight session, practitioners often engage in rituals to attune themselves to the energies of the Moon. This may involve meditation, grounding exercises, or the recitation of invocations to invoke the Moon's guidance. The scrying space is often set with intention, with candles, crystals, and other ritual tools arranged to create a conducive environment for the practice. The practitioner then enters a focused receptivity, allowing the Moonlight to guide their gaze into the scrying medium.

Interpreting the visions and impressions received during moonlight scrying requires a combination of intuition, symbolism, and personal insight. Practitioners may journal their experiences, noting the symbols, colors, or emotions that arise during the session. Over time, patterns and themes may emerge, offering more profound insights into the practitioner's psyche and the messages conveyed by the moonlit scrying sessions.

In conclusion, scrying by Moonlight is a mystical and ancient practice that weaves together the esoteric arts of divination with the ethereal energies of the Moon. Whether gazing into a crystal ball, a mirror, water, or flames, practitioners open themselves to the intuitive guidance and symbolic visions that emerge in the moonlit darkness. The Moon, as a silent witness to the dance of celestial energies, enhances the scrying experience, infusing it with a touch of enchantment and mystery. Through this ancient practice, people travel on a journey of self-discovery, connecting with the cosmic energies that regulate life's cycles and accessing their subconscious minds. Moonlight scrying transforms into a holy and intimate ritual, a dance between the visible and invisible, a voyage led by the Moon's bright presence.

Dream Interpretation and Moon Magic

Dream interpretation and moon magic form a symbiotic relationship, intertwining the mystical influence of the Moon with the enigmatic realm of dreams. Throughout history, cultures worldwide have recognized the Moon's profound impact on the human psyche, and many believe that the Moon holds the key to unlocking the secrets hidden within our dreams. Exploring this intricate connection allows individuals to delve into the rich tapestry of symbols, energies, and archetypes manifesting in their dreams, unlocking a pathway to self- discovery, intuition, and the potent world of moon magic.

Dreams have long been regarded as portals to the inner realms of the psyche, where the subconscious mind communicates in symbols, metaphors, and imagery. With its increasing luminosity, the waxing Moon is associated with growth, manifestation, and the initiation of new energies. Dreams during this phase may carry themes of beginnings, creativity, and the unveiling of hidden potential. The waxing crescent, leading to the full Moon, is a time when the energies of the subconscious are believed to align with the expansive forces of the Moon, offering glimpses into untapped aspects of the self.

Dreams may intensify as the Moon reaches its total luminescence and become more vivid. The full Moon is often linked to heightened emotions, illumination, and the revelation of truths. Dreams during this phase may bring forth insights, heightened intuition, or a deepening of emotional experiences. The full Moon's energy is thought to illuminate the hidden recesses of the subconscious, bringing clarity and revelation to the dreamer. It is a time when the veil between the conscious and unconscious realms is believed to thin, allowing for a more direct communion with the spiritual and intuitive aspects of the self.

Conversely, during the waning phases of the Moon, dreams may take on themes of release, reflection, and surrender. The waning Moon symbolizes a period of letting go, shedding old patterns, and making space for renewal. Dreams at this time may offer guidance on what needs to be released, bringing forth symbols and scenarios that reflect the process of surrender. The waning crescent, leading to the new Moon, is mainly associated with introspection, preparation for new beginnings, and the symbolic death and rebirth inherent in the lunar cycle.

In the realm of moon magic, practitioners often pay close attention to the lunar phases when interpreting their dreams. The lunar cycle becomes vital for understanding the energetic currents that influence the dream landscape. Dream journals, where individuals record their dreams alongside the corresponding lunar phases, serve as valuable repositories of insights into the intricate dance between the Moon and the dreamer's subconscious.

Moon magic also draws upon the archetypal symbolism associated with the Moon in various cultures. In mythology, the Moon is often linked to feminine energies, intuition, and the mysteries of the night. The moon goddess, represented as Selene, Luna, or other cultural variations, symbolizes the feminine principle, the unconscious, and the ever-changing cycles of life. In dreams, the appearance of the Moon or moon-related symbols may carry profound meaning, reflecting aspects of the dreamer's relationship with the feminine, intuition, or the cyclical nature of their journey.

Crystals, often integral to moon magic practices, may also find their way into dream interpretation. Placing crystals with lunar associations, such as moonstone or selenite, under the pillow or near the bed is believed to enhance dream recall, amplify intuitive insights, and facilitate a deeper connection with the energies of the Moon. The crystals act as conduits, channeling the lunar vibrations into the dream space and enhancing the dreamer's receptivity to symbolic messages.

Moon magic rituals, conducted with intention during specific lunar phases, can influence the dream realm. For example, a New Moon ritual focused on setting intentions and planting seeds of manifestation may carry its energy into the dream state, bringing forth dreams that align with the initiated intentions. Similarly, a Full Moon ritual centered on illumination and release may resonate in the dream landscape, offering insights into what needs to be brought to light and released for personal growth.

Lucid dreaming, a practice where the dreamer becomes aware of their dream state and may exert some control over the dream narrative, is another facet of moon magic and dream exploration. Some practitioners intentionally cultivate lucid dreaming during specific lunar phases, using techniques such as reality checks, affirmations, or meditation before sleep to enhance their awareness within the dream realm.

Moon magic and dream interpretation also share common ground in emphasizing intuition and symbolism. Both practices invite individuals to tap into their inner wisdom, trusting the intuitive insights that arise from the depths of the psyche. Symbols in dreams, whether influenced by the Moon or other archetypal energies, are regarded as a language of the soul. The Moon, as a powerful symbol itself, adds layers of depth and mystery to the symbolic messages that unfold in the dream realm. Interpreting these symbols becomes a journey of unraveling the personal mythology woven into the dreamer's subconscious.

Moon magic rituals, such as drawing down the Moon or invoking lunar energies, may be incorporated into dream incubation practices. Dreamers can set the intention to receive guidance, insights, or messages related to their moon magic work during the dream state. By aligning the dream intention with the lunar phases and incorporating ritualistic elements, individuals create a sacred bridge between their waking and dreaming realities, allowing the Moon's magic to permeate the dream landscape.

The practice of dream interpretation within the context of moon magic is a deeply personal and intuitive journey. It involves developing a nuanced understanding of one's dream language, recognizing recurring symbols, and deciphering the emotional tones embedded in the dream narratives. As dreamers attune themselves to the Moon's phases, they may notice patterns, themes, and energetic shifts that provide valuable insights into their emotional well-being, spiritual growth, and the cyclical nature of their journey.

Symbolism and the mystical influence of the Moon. As the moon waxes and wanes, it leaves its imprint on the dream landscape, influencing the themes, energies, and symbols that manifest during the dream state. The intricate dance between the Moon and dreams becomes a pathway to self-discovery, personal growth, and a deeper connection with the mysteries of the subconscious. Dreamers, guided by the luminous presence of the Moon, embark on a journey of exploration, unlocking the secrets hidden within the enigmatic realm of dreams and embracing the profound magic that unfolds when the Moonlight meets the landscapes of the night.

CHAPTER VIII

Crafting Moon Elixirs and Potions

Infusing Water with Lunar Energy

This sacred infusion process involves placing water in direct contact with Moonlight during specific lunar phases, creating a charged elixir that is believed to carry the energies of the Moon's cycle. The resulting lunar-infused water becomes a versatile tool in various spiritual and magical practices, offering a medium for intention setting, ritual purification, and energetic alignment with the celestial forces.

The lunar cycle, marked by the phases of the Moon, serves as a guide for infusing water with specific energies. Each lunar phase is thought to bring forth distinct qualities and influences, and practitioners often choose the phase that aligns with their intentions. For instance, during the waxing Moon, when the Moon is transitioning from new to complete, the energies are associated with growth, manifestation, and initiation. This phase is ideal for infusing water with intentions related to new beginnings, creativity, and the amplification of positive energies.

Conversely, the waning moon phase, from the full Moon to the new Moon, is linked to release, reflection, and surrender. This phase is chosen for infusing water with energies conducive to letting go of negativity, shedding old patterns, and preparing for renewal. As the Moon wanes, it is believed to draw out impurities and stagnant energies from the water, purifying it for intentional use. The

Full Moon, regarded as a peak of lunar energy, is a potent time for infusing water with the culmination of the

Moon's influence. The Full Moon carries energies of illumination, clarity, and heightened intuition. Water infused under the Full Moon is believed to absorb the maximum lunar energy, making it a potent elixir for spiritual practices, divination, and enhancing intuitive abilities. The Full Moon's radiant glow imparts a sense of completeness and fullness to the infused water.

To begin the process of infusing water with lunar energy, practitioners typically choose a clear glass or container to hold the water. Clear quartz crystals may be added to amplify the energies, as quartz is known for its ability to enhance and store energy. The container is then placed outdoors to be directly exposed to Moonlight. The moonlit water absorbs the subtle vibrations and energies associated with the specific lunar phase, creating a charged elixir.

Intention setting is a crucial aspect of infusing water with lunar energy. Before placing the water under the Moonlight, practitioners may hold the container and focus on their intentions, desires, or goals. This intentional energy is believed to be transferred to the water, creating a harmonious alignment between the lunar energies and the practitioner's purpose. Whether the intention is for personal growth, emotional healing, or spiritual insight, the infused water represents the practitioner's aspirations.

Infusing water with lunar energy is not only about the practical benefits of the charged water but also about creating a sacred and mindful ritual. As practitioners engage in this act, they are encouraged to be present, connecting with the natural world and the cosmic energies. The rhythmic cycles of the Moon become a mirror for the cyclical nature of life, offering an opportunity for reflection, renewal, and the conscious co-creation of one's reality.

Moon water, as the infused elixir is often called, can be incorporated into various spiritual and magical practices. In Wiccan traditions, moon water is considered a consecrated tool for rituals, spellwork, and altar offerings. It may be sprinkled or used to anoint candles, crystals, or ritual tools, infusing them with the lunar energies charged within the water. Moon water can also be added to bath rituals, creating a purifying and spiritually rejuvenating experience.

Drinking moon water is believed to enhance spiritual awareness, intuition, and overall well-being in holistic and metaphysical practices. As individuals consume the charged water, they absorb the subtle lunar energies, creating a harmonious resonance between their internal state and the external celestial influences.

Gardening enthusiasts often use moon water to water plants, believing it fosters growth, vitality, and resilience. The infused water, carrying the energies of the waxing Moon, is thought to support the germination and flourishing of plants. Moon water may also be incorporated into rituals or ceremonies performed in natural settings, creating a sacred connection between the practitioner, the Moon, and the elements of the Earth.

The use of moon water extends beyond individual practices to community and collective rituals. During significant lunar events, such as eclipses or rare celestial occurrences, groups may gather to collectively charge water with the intensified energies of the divine moment. This communal infusion becomes a shared experience, fostering a sense of unity, intention, and connection with the larger cosmic forces.

While infusing water with lunar energy is deeply rooted in spiritual and magical traditions, it also resonates with the broader awareness of the interconnectedness between humans and the natural world. It reflects a conscious acknowledgment of the Moon's influence on the Earth's rhythms, tides, and the intricate dance of life. By intentionally infusing water with lunar energy, individuals honor the timeless wisdom embedded in the cycles of the Moon and embrace a harmonious relationship with the celestial forces that shape their existence.

In conclusion, infusing water with lunar energy is a sacred and transformative practice that bridges the mystical influences of the Moon with intentional rituals. The lunar cycle becomes a guide, allowing practitioners to align their intentions with the specific energies of each phase. Whether used in personal rituals, spiritual practices, or communal ceremonies, moon water serves as a tangible conduit for the subtle vibrations of the Moon. Individuals engage in this intentional act and become active participants in the cosmic dance, harmonizing their energies with the celestial rhythms and unlocking the transformative power in the sacred alliance between water and the Moon.

Moon-Enhanced Herbal Brews

Moon-enhanced herbal brews represent a fusion of ancient herbal wisdom and the mystical energies of the Moon, creating elixirs that connect individuals with the cycles of nature and the celestial influences of the Moon. Herbal infusions have long been revered for their therapeutic properties, and when aligned with the phases of the Moon, they take on an additional layer of potency. The Moon, with its waxing and waning energies, is believed to influence the subtle qualities of herbs, enhancing their healing properties and creating a dynamic interplay between the natural world and cosmic forces. Whether used for relaxation, meditation, or ceremonial purposes, moon- enhanced herbal brews offer a holistic approach to well- being that harmonizes the medicinal properties of herbs with the cyclical rhythms of the Moon.

The practice of brewing herbal concoctions under the influence of the Moon is rooted in various cultural and spiritual traditions. Herbalism, the art of utilizing plants for medicinal and therapeutic purposes, recognizes the significance of lunar cycles in enhancing the efficacy of herbal remedies. The waxing Moon, associated with growth and vitality, is an opportune time for harvesting and preparing herbs for infusion. This phase is believed to accentuate the plants' life force and medicinal qualities, making it an ideal period for creating herbal brews that support physical health and well-being.

During the waxing Moon, herbalists may gather fresh herbs from gardens or wild spaces, selecting plants that align with their intended therapeutic effects. Conversely, refreshing herbs like peppermint or ginger might be chosen for teas designed to boost energy and vitality. The practitioner's intention and the specific properties of the selected herbs converge during the brewing process, creating a synergy believed to be amplified by the waxing Moon's energies.

As the Moon reaches its fullness, so does the potential of moon-enhanced herbal brews. The full Moon, a symbol of culmination and illumination, is a powerful time for infusing herbal concoctions with heightened energies. The infused water absorbs the full spectrum of lunar vibrations, creating elixirs that are not only therapeutic but also deeply connected to the spiritual and cosmic dimensions. Full Moon herbal brews become offerings to the psyche, aligning with the energies of illumination and insight. Herbalists may choose herbs that facilitate introspection, such as mugwort or sage, to craft teas that support divination practices or enhance spiritual experiences during meditation.

The waning moon phase, from the full Moon to the new Moon, invites a shift in focus from growth to release. Herbal brews created during this period may align with intentions related to detoxification, cleansing, and letting go of stagnant energies. Herbs with purifying properties, such as dandelion or nettle, are chosen to create teas that aid in eliminating toxins from the body and mind. The waning Moon's influence is believed to enhance the herbal infusion's ability to support individuals in releasing physical and emotional burdens.

The new Moon, a symbol of beginnings and renewal, marks the completion of the lunar cycle and the commencement of a new one. Herbalists may use this time to reflect on their intentions for the upcoming cycle and craft herbal brews that align with fresh starts and new endeavors. Teas made from herbs associated with new beginnings, like calendula or lemon balm, are believed to carry the energy of the new Moon, offering support for intention setting and goal manifestation.

The process of preparing moon-enhanced herbal brews involves a mindful and intentional approach. Practitioners often create a sacred space for the brewing ritual, infusing the process with reverence for the plants and the celestial energies. The choice of vessel, whether a ceramic teapot or a glass jar, becomes a symbolic container for capturing the essence of the Moon and the herbs. Clear quartz crystals, known for their amplifying properties, may be placed near the brewing vessel to enhance the infusion's energetic qualities.

Before beginning the brewing process, herbalists may engage in a brief meditation or grounding exercise, connecting with the energies of the Moon and attuning themselves to the plants' inherent wisdom. The herbs are then placed in the brewing vessel, and hot water is poured over them, initiating the infusion process. As the herbs steep, the practitioner may recite affirmations or invocations that align with their intentions for the brew. The moonlit night becomes a backdrop for this sacred alchemy, where the union of herbal wisdom and lunar energies transpires.

Moon-enhanced herbal brews are not only about the medicinal qualities of the herbs but also about the experiential and spiritual dimensions of the brewing ritual. Sipping a cup of moon-infused herbal tea becomes a moment of communion with nature's cycles and the cosmic dance of the Moon. Individuals may drink the brew mindfully, savoring each sip and allowing the subtle energies of the herbs and the Moon to permeate their being. This intentional consumption creates a holistic experience that nourishes the physical body, mind, and spirit.

Beyond individual rituals, moon-enhanced herbal brews find a place in collective ceremonies and celebrations. Moon circles or gatherings during significant lunar events may incorporate the brewing of herbal teas as a communal activity. Guided by the shared intention, participants contribute to creating a collective elixir that embodies the energies of the Moon and the combined qualities of the chosen herbs. Brewing and drinking together becomes a unifying experience, fostering community, connection, and alignment with the larger cosmic rhythms.

Moon-enhanced herbal brews are also placed in contemporary wellness practices, where individuals seek holistic approaches to self-care and balance. Integrative health enthusiasts recognize the benefits of herbal infusions for supporting physical health, emotional well-being, and spiritual growth. Moon-infused herbal teas are embraced not only for their therapeutic properties but also for their alignment with the natural cycles that govern life. The practice appeals to those who seek a deeper connection with nature, incorporating the wisdom of ancient traditions into modern lifestyles.

In conclusion, moon-enhanced herbal brews exemplify the harmonious integration of herbal wisdom and lunar energies, creating elixirs that resonate with nature's cycles and the Moon's celestial dance. The Moon's waxing, complete, and waning phases offer unique opportunities for infusing herbal concoctions with specific qualities and intentions. Moon-enhanced herbal brews, whether crafted for personal rituals, communal ceremonies, or holistic well- being, reflect a timeless practice that continues to bridge the realms of tradition, spirituality, and contemporary wellness.

Creating Moonlit Oils and Salves

Creating moonlit oils and salves is a sacred alchemical practice that draws on the potent energies of the Moon to infuse botanical essences with mystical properties. This ancient art, rooted in herbalism and esoteric traditions, recognizes the Moon as a celestial force that influences the natural world, tides, and the subtle energies within plants. By harnessing the luminous energies of the Moon during specific lunar phases, practitioners aim to enhance the therapeutic qualities of oils and salves, creating potions that serve not only as physical remedies but also as conduits for spiritual and energetic healing.

The choice of lunar phase plays a pivotal role in creating moonlit oils and salves. Each phase of the Moon is associated with unique energetic qualities, and practitioners carefully select the phase that aligns with their intentions. During its journey from new to complete, the waxing Moon is linked to growth, expansion, and the amplification of energies. This phase is ideal for creating oils and salves intended to promote healing, vitality, and the initiation of new endeavors. The waxing crescent, leading to the full Moon, becomes a potent period for harvesting and preparing herbs for infusion, as the Moon's increasing luminosity is believed to enhance the life force within plants.

The full Moon, with its peak illumination, is a focal point for creating moonlit oils and salves charged with the complete spectrum of lunar energies. The full Moon signifies culmination, clarity, and heightened intuition. Practitioners often select herbs associated with the specific qualities of the full Moon, such as mugwort or vervain, to infuse into oils and salves. The resulting concoctions are believed to carry the expansive and illuminating energies of the full Moon, making them powerful tools for spiritual practices, divination, and enhancing intuitive abilities.

Conversely, the waning moon phase, from full Moon to new Moon, is a time associated with release, purification, and surrender. Oils and salves created during this phase may focus on intentions related to letting go of negativity, banishing unwanted energies, and preparing for renewal. As the Moon wanes, it is thought to draw out impurities and stagnant energies from the plants, infusing the oils and salves with purifying qualities. The waning crescent, leading to the new Moon, becomes a period conducive to crafting blends that support introspection and the shedding of old patterns.

The new Moon, symbolizing beginnings and new possibilities, marks the completion of the lunar cycle and the start of a fresh one. Oils and salves created during this time may align with intentions for new ventures, personal growth, or the initiation of transformative processes. Practitioners may choose herbs associated with new beginnings, like calendula or jasmine, to infuse into oils and salves, capturing the energies of the new Moon for intention setting and manifestation.

Creating moonlit oils and salves involves a series of intentional and mindful steps. Herbalists often begin by selecting a carrier oil, such as jojoba or almond oil, to serve as the base for the infusion. Clear glass jars are commonly chosen as vessels for the process, allowing practitioners to observe the injection and the Moon's influence. The harvested or collected herbs, concerning their natural cycles, are added to the carrier oil in the jar.

Before exposing the oil to Moonlight, practitioners engage in a preparatory ritual. This may involve grounding exercises, invocations, or the recitation of affirmations to attune themselves to the energies of the Moon and the plants. The ritualistic elements give the procedure purpose and a stronger bond with the spiritual parts of the work. To enhance the energies, some practitioners add crystals associated with the moon, like moonstone or clear quartz, to the preparation.

The jar containing the oil and herbs is then placed in an outdoor space where it can be directly exposed to Moonlight. The choice of location may be influenced by the practitioner's spiritual beliefs or the specific qualities they wish to infuse into the oil. A windowsill, garden, or any open area where the Moon's rays can reach the jar suits the infusion process. The duration of exposure varies, with practitioners often leaving the oil to absorb Moonlight overnight, allowing it to undergo a complete lunar cycle.

Throughout the I fusion period, practitioners may revisit the jar, engaging in moments of reflection, meditation, or additional invocations. The intention set during the preparatory ritual is reinforced during these moments, creating a harmonious alignment between the practitioner's purpose and the energies of the moonlit infusion. The practitioner may also observe the subtle changes in the oil, noting any shifts in color, aroma, or energetic qualities that signify the integration of lunar energies.

Upon completion of the infusion process, the moonlit oil is strained to remove the herbal remnants, leaving a charged elixir ready for use. Some practitioners incorporate additional elements, such as essential oils or flower essences, to enhance the oil's therapeutic and energetic properties. The resulting moonlit oil becomes a versatile tool that can be applied to the skin, used in massage, added to bath rituals, or incorporated into spiritual practices.

Moonlit salves, a denser form of infused oils, involve the incorporation of beeswax or another solidifying agent to create a balm-like consistency. The process of creating moonlit salves mirrors that of oils, with the added step of melting the beeswax into the infused oil to achieve the desired texture. Salves are often preferred for topical applications, providing a concentrated form of the herbal and lunar energies. The solidified nature of salves makes them convenient for storage and easy to transport, allowing practitioners to carry the Moon's magic with them.

The apple actions of moonlit oils and salves span physical, emotional, and spiritual realms. The oils, charged with the energy of the Moon and the essence of the infused herbs, are believed to possess therapeutic properties that address specific health concerns. For example, Lavender-infused moonlit oil may promote relaxation and alleviate stress, while calendula-infused oil could support skin health and rejuvenation.

Beyond their physical applications, moonlit oils and salves serve as spiritual and energetic healing conduits. The intentional infusion of lunar energies creates elixirs that resonate with the subtle dimensions of existence. Practitioners may anoint themselves with moonlit oils during meditation, rituals, or ceremonies, using them to enhance their connection with the spiritual realms and amplify their intuitive abilities. The oils become integral to energy work, providing a tangible medium for attention setting, energy clearing, and chakra balancing.

Moonlit oils and salves are also embraced in holistic wellness practices that address mind, body, and spirit interconnectedness. The intentional blending of herbal wisdom, lunar energies, and personal intention aligns with the principles of holistic well-being. Individuals who seek a holistic approach to self-care and balance may incorporate moonlit oils and salves into their daily rituals, creating moments of mindfulness, connection with nature, and alignment with the cosmic rhythms.

In conclusion, creating moonlit oils and salves represents a convergence of herbal alchemy, lunar wisdom, and spiritual intention. The intentional infusion of oils with the energies of the Moon during specific lunar phases adds a dimension of magic and potency to these herbal concoctions. From the waxing to the full and waning moon phases, practitioners align their intentions with the unique qualities of each lunar cycle, creating oils and salves that serve as potent tools for physical, emotional, and spiritual well-being. As practitioners engage in this ancient art, they become active participants in cosmic dance, weaving together the earthly and celestial energies to create elixirs that carry the magic of the moonlit night.

CHAPTER IX

Moonlit Celebrations and Festivals

Honoring Lunar Deities

Honoring lunar deities is a sacred practice that spans cultures and civilizations, reflecting the profound significance of the Moon in human spirituality. Throughout history, the Moon has been revered as a celestial entity that influences the natural world, tides, and the ebb and flow of life. Lunar deities, associated with the Moon's mysterious and cyclical nature, are revered in religious pantheons, mythology, and spiritual practices worldwide. Through honoring these sacred beings, practitioners connect with the lunar energies in search of direction, favors, and a better comprehension of the cosmic forces that mold reality.

In various mythologies, the Moon is personified as a deity, often depicted as a god or god embodying the Moon's transformative phases. The archetype of the moon goddess is prevalent in diverse cultures, each presenting unique attributes and symbolism. In Greek mythology, Selene is the goddess of the Moon, representing the luminescent beauty of the night sky. Selene is often portrayed driving a chariot drawn by celestial horses across the heavens, illuminating the world below. Her Roman counterpart, Luna, shares similar locations, embodying the Moon's ethereal glow and influence on the nocturnal landscape.

In ancient Egyptian mythology, Thoth, the god of wisdom and knowledge, is linked to the Moon, serving as a guide through the mystical realms. Thoth's lunar associations extend to his role as the time measurer, emphasizing the

Moon's connection to cycles, seasons, and the cosmic order. Similarly, the Hindu tradition venerates Chandra, the moon god, symbolizing immortality and the rhythmic cycles of life and death. Chandra is often depicted with a soothing and compassionate presence, reflecting the Moon's gentle influence on emotions and the human psyche.

According to Norse mythology, the Moon is connected to Mani, a personification of the Moon's phases and the sibling of the sun goddess Sol. Mani, as the keeper of the Moon, rides across the night sky, steering a chariot drawn by a team of enchanted horses. This cosmic journey symbolizes the eternal dance between light and darkness, mirrored in the waxing and waning of the Moon. The Norse tradition acknowledges the Moon's intrinsic connection to the natural cycles of existence.

In Mesopotamian mythology, the moon god Sin is revered as the deity presiding over the Moon's influence on Earth. Sin is associated with wisdom, divination, and the cycles of time, embodying the lunar energies that shape the destinies of mortals. The worship of Sin reflects the acknowledgment of the Moon's role in illuminating hidden truths and guiding seekers on their spiritual journey.

Honoring lunar deities involves diverse rituals, ceremonies, and devotional practices that vary across cultures and spiritual traditions. These acts of reverence are designed to establish a sacred connection with the divine energies embodied by the Moon and its associated deities. Devotees may engage in moonlit ceremonies, offer prayers, or create altars adorned with symbols and representations of lunar entities. These rituals intend to attune oneself to the cosmic frequencies, seeking blessings, protection, and insights from the lunar realms. The phases of the Moon often dictate the timing of ceremonies dedicated to lunar deities. During the waxing Moon, when the lunar energies are rising, practitioners may focus on intentions related to growth, manifestation, and the pursuit of wisdom. This is a reasonable time for invocations, prayers, and offerings that align with the expansive forces associated with the waxing Moon. Rituals during this phase may emphasize personal and spiritual development, drawing inspiration from the increasing luminosity of the Moon. Conversely, the full Moon, with its peak illumination, is a pivotal time for honoring lunar deities. The full Moon is a mother of culmination, clarity, and heightened spiritual awareness. Devotees may engage in rituals that celebrate the divine presence of lunar entities, expressing gratitude, seeking guidance, or deepening their connection to the Moon's mystical energies. Full moon ceremonies often involve offerings of gratitude, meditation, and symbolic gestures that honor the goddess or god associated with the Moon.

The waning moon phase, from the full Moon to the new Moon, is a time for release, purification, and surrender. Devotees may help us let go of negative energies, old patterns, or obstacles that hinder their spiritual progress. Rituals during this phase may involve energy clearing, divination, or meditation to align with the transformative energies associated with the waning Moon. Honoring lunar deities during this time invites their guidance in shedding old layers and preparing for renewal.

The new Moon, symbolizing beginnings and the start of a new lunar cycle, offers devotees an opportunity for fresh starts, setting intentions, and planting the seeds of new endeavors. Rituals during the new moon phase may involve prayers for guidance, manifestation, and blessings from lunar deities. Devotees may seek the support of the Moon's energies in initiating projects, embarking on new spiritual paths, or nurturing the seeds of intentions that will unfold during the subsequent lunar phases.

In Wiccan and Pagan traditions, the worship of lunar deities often involves the creation of sacred circles, invocations, and ceremonial practices that align with the phases of the Moon. Drawing upon the correspondences between the Moon's energies and the elements, practitioners may incorporate rituals such as drawing down the Moon – a practice where the divine essence of the moon goddess is invoked into the practitioner – to facilitate a direct connection with the lunar entities. Offerings of crystals, flowers, or symbolic representations of the Moon are commonly included in these rituals as acts of reverence and devotion.

Cultivating a relationship with lunar deities extends beyond formal rituals, encompassing daily practices that acknowledge the Mo's presence in one's life. Individuals express their reverence for lunar energies by observing the moonrise or moonset, creating moon water by leaving water under the Moonlight or simply contemplating silently under the night sky. Many practitioners also incorporate lunar symbols into their daily lives, wearing moonstone jewelry, adorning altars with lunar imagery, or incorporating lunar cycles into meditation practices.

The symbolic associations of lunar deities are rich with meaning and offer a tape try of archetypal energies for devotees to explore. The Moon's cyclical journey mirrors the ebb and flow of life, death, and rebirth, embodying the eternal dance between light and darkness. Lunar deities often encapsulate the duality inherent in this cosmic dance, symbolizing the nurturing, receptive, and intuitive aspects of the feminine alongside the illuminating, guiding, and protective qualities associated with the masculine.

The symbolic resonance of lunar deities extends beyond mythology, permeating various aspects of human culture and spiritual expression. In art, literature, and poetry, the Moon and its deities are metaphors for the mysteries of existence, the passage of time, and the cyclical nature of life. The Moon's influence on human emotions, creativity, and intuition has inspired countless works of art, capturing the essence of the Moon's ethereal beauty and spiritual significance.

In conclusion, honoring lunar deities is a timeless practice that invites individuals to connect with the celestial forces that shape the tapestry of existence. Devotees seek to establish a sacred relationship with the Moon and its associated deities through formal rituals, daily observances, or symbolic gestures. The diverse expressions of lunar worship across cultures underscore the universal recognition of the Moon's influence on spiritual, emotional, and cosmic dimensions. As practitioners engage in acts of reverence, they participate in the ancient dance between Earth and sky, honoring the luminous energies that have guided humanity's spiritual journey throughout the ages.

Seasonal Moon Festivals

Seasonal Moon Festivals are rich tapestries weaving into the cultural and spiritual fabric of diverse societies, reflecting a harmonious dance between human existence and the cosmic rhythms of the moon. These festivals, rooted in ancient traditions and agricultural cycles, celebrate the changing seasons and the cyclical journey of the Moon across the night sky. Found in cultures worldwide, these celebrations are marked by rituals, ceremonies, and communal gatherings that go through the lunar phases, connecting individuals with the profound interconnectedness of the Earth, the Moon, and the cycles of life.

One of the most widely recognized seasonal moon festivals is the Mid-Autumn Festival, celebrated in many East Asian cultures. Known by various names such as Chuseok in Korea, Tsukimi in Japan, and Zhōngqiū Jié in China, this festival typically occurs in September or October during the full Moon. Central to the Mid-Autumn Festival is the appreciation of the Moon's beauty and the bountiful harvest. F families come together for feasts, moon-viewing parties, and the sharing of mooncakes, a traditional pastry often filled with sweet bean paste or lotus seed paste. Lanterns are lit, symbolizing the illumination of one's inner self, and folktales about the Moon's enchanting powers are shared. The festival reflects themes of reunion, gratitude, and the cyclical nature of life.

In India, the Sharad Purnima Festival illuminates the night of the full Moon in October. This celebration is deeply connected to the autumn harvest and is considered auspicious for spiritual practices. Devotees engage in various rituals, including fasting, singing devotional songs, and participating in activities that symbolize celebrating life's abundance. The full Moon during Sharad Purnima is believed to possess unique qualities, and individuals often spend the night praying and meditating, seeking blessings for health, prosperity, and spiritual growth.

The Harvest Moon Festival holds cultural significance in the Western world, especially in agricultural communities. Communal gatherings, feasts, and expressions of gratitude for the abundance of the harvest season mark the festival. In some cultures, traditional folk dances and music accompany the festivities, adding a joyful dimension to the celebration of nature's bounty.

These vibrant lanterns symbolize the overcoming of darkness and the triumph of light. Families participate in various activities, including solving riddles on lanterns, enjoying traditional performances, and releasing sky lanterns into the night sky. The festival's culmination aligns with the first full Moon of the lunar year, creating a splendid visual spectacle.

Tribes such as the Algonquin, Ojibwe, and Dakota honor this occasion with ceremonies, dances, and communal feasts. The Strawberry Moon holds spiritual significance, and rituals during this festival often include praising the Earth for its bounty and seeking blessings for the growing season ahead. The festival encapsulates a deep connection to nature and the recognition of the Moon as a guide for seasonal activities.

During this enchanting festival, people release decorated floating baskets, or krathongs, onto rivers and waterways, symbolizing letting go of negativity and honoring the water goddess. The soft glow of candles and lanterns on the water creates a mesmerizing spectacle, reflecting the Moon's radiance. Loy Krathong is a time for reflection, purification, and renewing one's spirit as the water carries away symbolic burdens.

The Poya Festival in Sri Lanka is celebrated on each full moon, known as Poya day, throughout the lunar calendar. With a predominantly Buddhist population, the festival holds religious significance, marking critical events in the life of Siddhartha Gautama, who later became the Buddha. On Poya days, Buddhists engage in spiritual practices, visit temples, and participate in acts of charity. The full Moon is seen as a symbol of enlightenment, and the festival provides an opportunity for reflection, meditation, and cultivating virtues.

The sighting of the new moon, which marks the beginning of fasting, prayer, and introspection, marks the beginning of the holy month of Ramadan in Islamic tradition. The lunar calendar determines the start and conclusion of Ramadan, where the new Moon marks the beginning of a new month. When Muslims gather to celebrate the joyous event of Eid al-Fitr, the sighting of the new Moon, sometimes referred to as the hill, is a moment of celebration and the conclusion of fasting. The Moon is the celestial timekeeper that determines the Islamic calendar's significant events and religious observances.

These Seasonal Moon Festivals illustrate the universal human impulse to celebrate and harmonize with the rhythms of nature. The Moon, with its ever-changing phases, serves as a celestial guide, influencing cultural traditions, religious practices, and the agricultural cycles that sustain communities. Each festival carries unique artistic expressions while sharing common themes of gratitude, renewal, and reverence for the interconnectedness of life.

In contemporary times, Seasonal Moon Festivals continue to evolve, adapting to the complexities of modern life while preserving their cultural and spiritual essence. Globalization and increased cultural exchange have led to the blending of traditions, with people from different backgrounds incorporating elements of various Seasonal Moon Festivals into their celebrations. Festivals that once held regional significance now resonate across orders, fostering a shared appreciation for the Moon's influence on human culture.

In conclusion, Seasonal Moon Festivals serve as timeless expressions of human connection to the natural world and the celestial cycles that shape our existence. These celebrations, rooted in ancient traditions, continue to weave threads of cultural identity, spiritual reverence, and communal harmony. Whether illuminated by lanterns, marked by harvest feasts, or observed through quiet reflection, Seasonal Moon Festivals offer a tapestry of diverse celebrations that honor the deep connection between humanity and the moon's cosmic dance.

Hosting Your Own Moonlit Gatherings

Hosting Your Own Moonlit Gatherings is a transformative and enchanting endeavor that allows individuals to create meaningful connections with nature, the cosmos, and their community. Moonlit gatherings, whether held in celebration of specific lunar phases or under the radiant glow of a full moon, offer a unique opportunity to harness the mystical energies of the night and weave them into communal experiences. Whether you are drawn to the spiritual, cultural, or aesthetic aspects of moonlit gatherings, organizing such events can be rewarding and magical.

Setting the stage for a moonlit gathering begins with choosing the correct location. Whether it's a backyard, a park, or a beach, selecting a space that allows for an unobstructed view of the Moon enhances the overall experience. Natural settings with open skies contribute to the ambiance, creating an immersive environment where participants can connect with the celestial energies.

Timing is critical in moonlit gatherings, with the lunar calendar as a guide. Choosing a date that aligns with a specific lunar phase, such as the full Moon or a new moon, adds an intentional dimension to the gathering. Each lunar phase carries unique energies, allowing hosts to tailor the event's theme or activities to align with the qualities associated with that phase.

Creating a focal point for the gathering adds a touch of magic and symbolism. Consider setting up a moon altar adorned with lunar symbols, crystals, and candles. This serves as a visual anchor, drawing participants into the enchanting atmosphere and inviting them to engage with the energies of the Moon. Incorporating elements such as moonstone, quartz crystals, or silver-colored objects enhances the connection to lunar vibrations.

Mo-lit rituals can infuse the gathering with purpose and spiritual depth. Depending on the lunar phase, rituals may include intention-setting ce monies, guided meditations, or symbolic activities that align with the energies of the Moon. For example, during a moon gathering, participants might write down what they wish to release and then burn the papers in a ceremonial fire, symbolizing letting go and renewal.

Food and drink offerings can elevate the moonlit gathering experience. Consider creating a menu containing ingredients associated with lunar energies, such as white or silver-colored foods, melons, or foods traditionally enjoyed during moon festivals worldwide. Moon-shaped cookies, lunar-inspired cocktails, or a communal feast add a festive element to the gathering.

The space's lighting plays a crucial role in enhancing the moonlit ambiance. Opt for soft, ambient lighting such as string lights, lanterns, or candles to create a natural glow. This not only adds to the enchantment of the gathering but also ensures visibility without overpowering the natural radiance of the Moon.

Incorporating music or soundscapes inspired by the Moon enhances the sensory experience. Soft instrumental tunes, ambient sounds of nature, or even drum circles can complement the mood, creating a multisensory journey that aligns with the lunar energies. Encourage participants to bring their instruments, fostering a collaborative and harmonious atmosphere.

Hosting moonlit gatherings allows participants to attune themselves to the natural rhythms of the night. Guided stargazing sessions, constellation identification, or storytelling about lunar myths and legends can deepen the connection to the celestial realm. Educating participants about the cultural and spiritual significance of the Moon in various traditions adds a layer of enrichment to the gathering.

Promoting a sense of inclusivity and community is fundamental to the success of moonlit gatherings. Encourage participants to share their stories, traditions, or experiences related to the Moon. This exchange of perspectives fosters a sense of unity and diversity, creating a tapestry of shared connections under the celestial canopy.

Engaging in mindful practices, such as m only yoga or meditation, invites participants to connect with their inner selves and the inner ies of the Moon. These activities promote a sense of tranquility, grounding, and spiritual reflection. A guided meditation focused on lunar energies or a moonlit yoga session under the open sky amplifies overall well-being.

For those seeking a more lighthearted atmosphere, incorporating creative activities adds an element of playfulness to the gathering. Moonlit crafting sessions, where participants create lunar-themed art or decorations, offer a chance for self-expression and contribute to the communal ambiance. Making a collaborative art installation, such as a moon mandala, allows participants to contribute their creative energy to the gathering.

Having successful communication is crucial to the success of moonlit events. Inform attendees in advance about the gathering's goal, subject, and schedule of events. Provide suggestions for attire, encourage the use of lunar-inspired accessories, and communicate any logistical details such as parking, seating arrangements, or specific items to bring.

M-only gatherings are not limited to specific cultural or spiritual traditions; they are open to interpretation and adaptation based on the host's and participants' preferences and beliefs. The key is to create an atmosphere that encourages connection, reflection, and a sense of wonder under the luminous embrace of the Moon.

In conclusion, hosting your moonlit gatherings is a venture into magic, spirituality, and communal connection. Whether guided by celestial intentions, cultural traditions, or simply a desire to bask in the beauty of the Moon, these gatherings offer a platform for shared experiences, creative expressions, and a deepened connection to the cosmic energies that weave through the night sky. As hosts curate an environment that honors the Moon's influence, participants embark on self-discovery, community building, and a harmonious dance under the moonlit heavens.

CONCLUSION

In conclusion, "Moonlit Beginnings: Spellcraft and Rituals for Lunar Novices - A Practical Handbook for Moon Magic" is a comprehensive and illuminating guide that beckons novices into the enchanting realm of moon magic. Throughout the pages of this book, readers are welcome to set off on an adventure that goes beyond the mundane, delving into the mystical and ancient practices associated with harnessing the power of the moon. By demystifying lunar magic, the e-book equips novices with practical knowledge, insightful rituals, and spells that embrace the inherent connection between the moon, nature, and the energies surrounding us.

The e-book emphasizes the importance of understanding the moon's phases and aligning magical practices with the lunar cycle. From new moon intentions to full moon manifestations, the handbook provides a roadmap for novices to synchronize their spellcraft with the celestial dance of the moon. The rituals and spells presented are not merely instructions but gateways to a deeper connection with the natural rhythms of the universe.

Furthermore, the e-book strongly emphasizes intention setting and mindfulness in moon magic. It encourages readers to approach spellcraft with reverence and a sense of purpose, fostering a mindful engagement with the energies they seek to invoke. By incorporating meditation, visualization, and intention elements into lunar rituals, novices are guided toward a more profound and meaningful practice.

Notably, "Moonlit Beginnings" encourages novices to explore their unique path within the realm of moon magic. It serves as a springboard for personal creativity and intuition, emphasizing that the moon's magic is a deeply personal and subjective experience. Readers are invited to adapt and personalize the rituals and spells, fostering a sense of ownership and authenticity in their magical journey.

In essence, "Moonlit Beginnings" is more than a handbook; it is a gateway to a world where the mystical energies of the moon become accessible to novices. As readers take in the knowledge found within, they become proficient in moon magic and establish a connection with the long-standing customs that have honored the moon throughout history. For individuals looking to embrace the enchanted world of lunar magic and start their moonlit beginnings, the e-book is an excellent resource because of its helpful advice, insightful analysis, and powerful style.

Thank you for buying and reading/listening to our book. If you found this book useful/helpful please take a few minutes and leave a review on the platform where you purchased our book. Your feedback matters greatly to us.

www.ingramcontent.com/pod-product-compliance
Lightning Source LLC
LaVergne TN
LVHW010346070526
838199LV00065B/5796